ALAS, BABYl

CW00433765

STUDIES IN REVELᴀᴛᴜᴏɴ 18

WM. L. TURNER

COPYRIGHT 2016

AUTHOR'S PREFACE

In December, 2006, my son-in-law, Rev. Jaime Sicairos, asked me to present a series of
studies in Revelation at North Harrison Independent Baptist Church in Ramsey, Indiana, where he was pastor. I agreed to do so, assuming the studies would take only a few weeks, and began the series on the first Wednesday night in January, 2006. The most recent war between Israel and Lebanon had concluded only a few weeks before, and interest in end time events was high.

What I had not realized was that the internet had now made vastly more resources available than there had been during the five previous times that I had given studies in Revelation, during my half century of ministry. As a result, rather than lasting only a few weeks, the study continued until mid-October, 2014.

In April, 2008 - I had by then gotten to chapter eleven - I suffered a near fatal accident one Wednesday evening on my way to church. After spending 112 days in four different hospitals, I was able, in September of that year, to resume teaching Revelation. During those months of recuperation, I came to believe that God had spared my life so that, among other things, I could complete the study of Revelation, and I kept at it for an additional six years.

Because these studies represented more than four thousand hours of research, I was asked to make them available in written form. After considerable hesitation about undertaking a task of that magnitude at the age of 70, I have resolved to do so, God willing and enabling me to complete the work. This series of messages, on what I found to be one of the most challenging portions of the book, chapter 18, is the beginning of a longer work that will hopefully cover the entire book.

It is my hope that readers will find in helpful in understanding this most timely portion of Scripture, in these last days in which we live. *Soli Deo gloria. Laudetur! Jesus Christus in Aeternum!*

Rev. 17:15-19

We return today, for the final time, to the 17th chapter of Revelation. We've been studying this chapter for about two months now. When we began our study of chapter 17, I told you it was both the most important chapter of the book, and also the most difficult to understand; and I also said that unless we get this chapter right, we're not going to understand the rest of the book.

So we've plowed through it for 2 months or so, and I've tried my best to give it a fair reading and explain what each of the symbols means. I hope we've succeeded in explaining it correctly, and comprehensibly, understandably. We have one verse yet to go, the final verse, verse 18; and then we can go on over to chapter 18, which is the dirge, the people mourning over Babylon's fall. So we'll start in, and see how far we get.

Last week we looked at verses 16-17, and saw the fate that awaits the whore, Babylon, which I've told you, and reiterate, represents the world system. More of that, I'll say more about her identity in just a moment. But verse 17 contains some extremely graphic language. It says that the ten kings, the ten nation confederacy which is supporting Antichrist, "Shall hate the whore, and shall make her desolate and naked, and shall devour her flesh, and shall burn her with fire."

I suggested that, in John's day, that is what the pagan, uncivilized peoples would do to the soldiers of the conquered army - they'd not only kill them, but they'd eat their bodies. And I think I talked about Captain Cook and the original inhabitants, the natives of Hawaii. So this pictures anarchy within Antichrist's domain; which often occurs in a country which is ready to collapse. Think of the French Revolution or the Russian Revolution, for example. In like manner, Antichrist's kingdom is falling into disarray, to make ready for the battle of Armageddon, where he is finally and forever defeated.

So the world's cultural, and economic, and educational system is swept away, and Antichrist sets up a regime of raw military might. I suggested that that's where most revolutions end up - the French Revolution produced Napoleon; the Russian Revolution produced Lenin and Stalin; the Chinese Revolution produced Mao Tse-tung. I also suggested that's where the current regime in Washington is headed.

Then we noted that it was God who put it in their hearts to do so, and to fulfill His will. The verb is in the active voice - He didn't just stand aside and allow them to destroy themselves - He caused it to happen. I spoke about the doctrines of predestination and free will, and insisted that, whatever may be the case with other people, these particular folks didn't have any free will - God caused them to destroy themselves.

Anyhow, that's some of what we talked about last week. Now today, I want you to look at verse 18: "And the woman which thou sawest is that great city, which reigneth over the kings of the earth."

John has given us the identity of the Beast - which is, Antichrist, the political and military system. He now identifies Babylon, the whore. And it says that she represents a city. What city? The city is not named; but it says the city "reigneth over the kings of the earth." As in other places, the Greek contains a play on words that doesn't translate readily into English. The word rendered "reigneth" is the same as the word for "kings" - the Greek word is "*basilea*" - so that it says, essentially, that she's the "king of the kings of the earth."

The puzzle, the challenge, is, of course, to determine what "city" is meant. I've observed before, that John was presumably writing under the watchful eye of a Roman censor, and if they didn't like what he was writing, the letter would never get delivered. They do the same thing in prisons today - and perhaps with good reason. They open your mail and read it, and if they don't like what it says, the letter never arrives, or else arrives in a redacted form - *i.e.,* they take out the parts they find objectionable.

So John was hiding his meaning in a symbol, that would have been readily apparent to his readers, who were familiar with the Jewish scriptures, but would have meant nothing to the Romans, who had never read the Old Testament. Several answers to the question have been proposed. Verse 9 refers to the "seven mountains, on which the woman sitteth." And because Rome was known as the City of Seven Hills, it's claimed that John was identifying the city as Rome, and predicting its destruction - which, of course, he couldn't say in so many words.

And that might have been the first thing that would have come to the minds of the original readers - although the "seven hills" upon which Rome sits, are certainly not "mountains", in any sense of the word. What we have around here are "hills"; what they have in eastern Kentucky are "mountains" - and there's a considerable difference. But leaving that aside, if we assumed that Rome was the city meant, we have to decide whether he means pagan Rome, of papal Rome, *i.e.,* the Roman Catholic Church.

Not surprisingly, Catholic writers think it refers to the pagan Roman empire, which was converted to Christianity in 313 A.D. The Reformation writers, who were being persecuted by the Catholics, saw it as being papal Rome - the popes, and the Roman Catholic Church. The problem is, if you adopt either one of those views, the present age did not end, and Jesus Christ did not return, either in 476 A.D., when the Roman Empire fell, nor at the time of the Protestant Reformation.

And so, while the older commentaries, Matthew Henry, Adam Clarke, Albert Barnes, Jamieson Fawsett and Brown, and others, claim that the Roman Catholic Church is meant, that view has now fallen into disfavor, and not many commentators hold that view today. If it does not mean either pagan Rome, or papal Rome, a third possibility is that it means the literal city of Babylon. The city of Babylon evidently existed in apostolic times, since Peter mentions "the church at Babylon" in his First Epistle, although by then Babylon was no longer an important city. The problem is, however, that the city of Babylon no longer exists; the site where it stood is in

Iraq, not too far from the present capital city of Baghdad; but the site of Babylon is a ruin; there hasn't been a city there for centuries.

Some writers insist that, in order that this prophecy might be fulfilled, the city of Babylon is going to be rebuilt in the last days. Bullinger predicted this in his commentary on Revelation, about a hundred years ago; and more recently, Hal Lindsey, who has a weekly broadcast on TBN, believes that Babylon is going to be rebuilt. There is, however, no indication that anyone has any intention of actually doing so.

The fourth possibility, and the one which I favor, is that Babylon stands for the entire world system. One commentator says that Babylon "represents all that is of the world." I've mentioned that before, of course, and you may wonder why I'm repeating it. The reason is, that the next chapter, chapter 18, sets out a dirge, a lament, the merchants wailing, over the fall of Babylon; and if we don't know what "Babylon" represents, chapter 18 isn't going to make any sense to us. And I'll say, right up front, that chapter 18, like chapter 17, is one that gets ignored by most preachers and churches. I've told you, several times, that I've never heard a sermon from Revelation 17, in 60 years of hearing preaching. I've never heard one from chapter 18, either. I suppose one reason that preachers skip over it is because they don't want to take the trouble to figure out exactly what it means.

So, before we tackle chapter 18, I want to make sure we've got this concept nailed down. Charles Dickens wrote a novel set at the time of the French Revolution; the title was "The Tale of Two Cities" - the two cities in question being London and Paris. Revelation is also a tale of two cities. In the third chapter of Revelation, in the sixth of the seven letters to the churches - the letter to Philadelphia, which symbolizes the persecuted church of the last days - He speaks of "the city of my God, which is new Jerusalem, which cometh down out of heaven from God." Rev. 3:12.

Then, after John has witnessed the destruction of the world system, he writes, in chapter 21 and verse 2: "And I John saw the holy city, new Jerusalem, coming down from God out of heaven, prepared as a bride adorned for her husband." Other references to the heavenly Jerusalem, the city of God, occur in Psalm 46: 4; Psalm 87:3; Hebrews 12:22; and Revelation 22:19. So one city John is writing about is the city of God, of which we'll have more to say when we get to chapters 21 and 22.

But John also describes another city, Babylon, which is here called "that great city." In the book of Jonah, the city of Nineveh, which God was threatening to destroy, is repeatedly called "that great city." In Jer. 22:8. God is threatening to destroy Jerusalem, if they don't repent, and Jeremiah refers to Jerusalem as "this great city." The phrase "great city" occurs 17 times in the King James Version, and the first 16 of those times, beginning in Genesis and ending in Revelation, 16 of the 17 refer to cities that God is fixing to destroy; the 17th, and final time it occurs is in Rev. 21:10, where it's speaking of heaven, right after where I read you a minute ago.

The first time the phrase occurs in the book of Revelation is in chapter 11, verse 8, where the two witnesses have just been killed, and it says: "And their dead bodies shall lie in the street of the great city, which spiritually is called Sodom and Egypt, where also our Lord was crucified."

So the "great city" spoken of here, is compared, likened to 4 other cities of the Bible - Sodom, Egypt, Babylon, and Jerusalem. Babylon, of course, was a city, the mention of which aroused strong feelings in the heart of every Jew of John's time, even though the Roman censor may have only regarded it as a small town out at the edge of the Empire.

It's compared to Sodom, the city which God destroyed with fire and brimstone because of their sexual perversion. Bro. Ron spoke at some length about Sodom last Wednesday night, and I'll not belabor the point; but isn't it interesting to note that today, in our own time, for the first time in at least two millenia, sodomy's been recognized as an acceptable alternative lifestyle; sodomites are regarded as a persecuted minority who have certain civil rights; and that doctrine is being shoved down the throats of gullible young people by the demonic public schools. And if saying that means we're dabbling into politics, so be it. It's a legitimate moral concern, about which the Bible speaks plainly, and concerning which churches ought to take a stand.

But the clear implication is that Antichirst's kingdom will, like Sodom, be a place of sexual perversion, where sexual sin is approved, and runs unchecked. So, I repeat, it's interesting to note that in our own day, for the first time in at least 2000 years, Sodomy has been legalized, and Sodomites have been considered a protected minority, allowed to marry, and to adopt children. There's never been any other society in history that recognized homosexual marriage, or allowed them to adopt children. Is that simply coincidence? Or is it the fulfillment of Bible prophecy?

Antichrist's kingdom is also compared to Egypt, the land in which the children of Israel had been enslaved for 400 years. So it's implying that Antichrist's kingdom will not only be a place of sexual perversion, but a place which will persecute Israel.

It's also compared to Jerusalem, the city where our Lord was crucified - as John well knew, since he was there, and had watched it happen. So it implies that Antichrist's kingdom will also be the enemy of Jesus Christ, and will persecute his followers.

But the most telling, most meaningful, most emotionally charged comparison, for John's readers would have been comparing Antichrist's kingdom to Babylon. As I say, while the city of Babylon still existed at the time John wrote this letter to the churches, it was no longer a town of any particular importance. But the Jews all knew what had happened there.

Babylon was, first of all, a place of great military power and oppression. They had, after all, come and conquered the Southern Kingdom, the nation of Judah, not just once, but twice - first in 606 B.C., and then again in 586 B.C. Babylon did so at a time when the Southern Kingdom had not been conquered for more than 400 years. That's longer than since the Pilgrims landed at Plymouth Rock. And so it suggests, as I've already said, that Antichrist will reign, not by the force of persuasion or ideas, not as the result of free and fair elections, but by raw military might.

Babylon had also been, for the Jews, a place of exile and alienation. The folks there worshiped different gods; they spoke a different language. The Jews were strangers there. There's a controversy raging at the moment about the Mexicans and other Hispanic immigrants; and much of the objection is, they're not like us - they're aliens - and they don't want to become assimilated into out culture. It's a debate which I'm much aware of, of course, since I have a Mexican son-in-law, four grandchildren who are half Mexican, and a fifth who is one-quarter Puerto Rican.

The Jews were like that in Babylon. We read in Psalm 137: "By the rivers of Babylon, there we sat down, yea, we wept, when we remembered Zion . . . How shall we sing the Lord's song in a strange land?" They definitely didn't want to assimilate.

It's certainly been true that the church of Jesus Christ has always been a pilgrim church - strangers in this world, in the world but not of it. I've sung you the song before, written about 100 years ago: "I am a stranger here within a foreign land; My home is far away, upon a golden strand." And more recently there's been a song: "This world is not my home, I'm just a-passing through." Indeed, Christians are commanded not to assimilate. Paul wrote to the Corinthians, II Cor. 6:17: "Wherefore, come out from among them, and be ye separate, saith the Lord."

And that's a theme we used to hear a lot about in fundamental churches, thirty years ago. I wrote my doctoral thesis about Christian schools; and in the course of my investigation, I collected dozens, if not hundreds, of Christian school handbooks. Every single one had a long section about "Christian separation." If you're going to be part of our Christian school, there are certain things other kids do, that you can't do. Heard any preaching along that line, lately?

And I will say, as an aside, that that's one reason I think Christian parents shouldn't put their kids in the public schools. One of the principal goals of public school education is to get the kids to assimilate - to share the world's philosophy, adopt its values, imitate its lifestyle - which is the direct opposite of what the Bible commands Christians, and Christian young people, to do.

I've already mentioned I Peter 5:13, where Peter speaks of "the church in Babylon." Now, if there really were a literal church, an organized body of believers, in the literal city of Babylon, at the time Peter was writing, it's the only place in the New Testament where we read anything about it. Some commentators think that, by the phrase, Peter simply was referring to the church, to believers, in general, and that he was saying, but laying it between the lines, so a Roman censor wouldn't get the point, and think it was a seditious statement, that the church in this present world is like the Jews in Babylon - foreigners, strangers, pilgrims, in the world but not of it, and someone who's looking for a city - as the author of Hebrews aptly stated it.

This will especially be true of those who have been saved during the tribulation, and to the Jews, during the tribulation, who are trapped in Antichrist's kingdom, and who are in effect given the choice: conform, or die.

And yet, although this world is enemy territory, and we're surrounded by God's enemies, it is a place where one who has the eye of faith can nonetheless see the glory of God. Some of the most profound visions in the Old Testament were given to Ezekiel - and as we've gone through Revelation, we've referred repeatedly to things Ezekiel wrote - the book of Ezekiel seems to have been much on John's mind when he was writing Revelation.

And Ezekiel begins his prophecy with these words: "Now it came to pass in the thirtieth year, in the fourth month, in the fifth day of the month, as I was among the captives by the river Chebar, that the heavens were opened, and I saw visions of God." Although we are here, in Satan's territory, surrounded by God's enemies, we can still hear the voice of God, as Ezekiel did, if we're listening for it. And you're much more likely to hear the voice of God if you're at his house, than if you're home watching American Idol.

Lest we should miss the point, John writes in the fourth verse of the next chapter, Chapter 18: "And I heard another voice from heaven, saying, Come out of her, my people, that ye be not partakers of her sins, and that ye receive not of her plagues." So the call for Christian separation is very definitely one of the themes of this section of the book.

Let me read you a couple of sentences from the "New Interpreters Bible," which is a liberal commentary, written about 10 years ago, and with which I don't usually agree. But see if you think they express this particular point well. Commenting on this point, they say:

"John writes and readers read in the mist of the dominion of the beast and Babylon's luxurious consumption. However strong the desire of the saints to come out from the midst of Babylon, the book of Revelation is addressed to people who breathe Babylon's ethos, whether they like it or not, and need a vision of how to live under its imperial rule yet without becoming a part of it. There is no escape from exile this side of the millennium, except, that is, in the difference of perspective that comes with a vision of a common life based on differing values."

And it that regard, he references Daniel, who would not defile himself with the king's meat, and the three Hebrew children, who would not worship Nebuchadnezzar's statue. They were trying to maintain their religious values, in the face of an alien culture that demanded they renounce God. You will also recall that the three Hebrew children got thrown into the fiery furnace, as a result. It takes much less than that to keep most folks away from church on Sunday morning, in our own day.

And with that, I think I'm going to leave it. As I said at the beginning, I consider this the most critical chapter in the book of Revelation; and I hope I've done it justice. I hope I've helped to clarify its meaning, rather than simply adding to your confusion. I also hope that what I've said will encourage you to study the chapter on your own, and seek to determine its meaning for yourself, instead of simply taking my word for it.

Next week, we'll begin chapter 18 - the dirge, the lament, of the merchants of Babylon over her destruction. As I said of chapter 17, so I also say of chapter 18, you've probably never heard a sermon from this chapter - I haven't, except the ones I''ve preached myself. So if you miss our study of it, you may never get another chance to hear it explained. That's why I hope you'll come back next Wednesday night, and bring some other folks with you.

Rev. 18:1-8

Tonight we begin our consideration of Revelation 18. We completed Revelation 17 last week, after spending a number of weeks studying the chapter which, I told you, was the most important, and also the most difficult, in the entire book, and which I considered the key to the book. I'm not going to spend a lot of time repeating what I said about the chapter - most of you were here for all, or at least the biggest part, of that study.

I'll simply note that, at the beginning of chapter 17, John sees a woman riding on a scarlet colored beast. And then the angel explains who the beast is, at some length - and we saw that he represents Anti-Christ; and then, in the last verse of the chapter, verse 18, he explains what the woman represents. He saves that until last, because it leads into what we've just read from chapter 18 - which is all about the woman, Babylon.

I explained last week that there are several different views of exactly who or what Babylon represents. The Catholic writers think she represents pagan Rome. The Protestant Reformation writers believed she represented the Roman Catholic Church. There is a third school of interpretation, Hal Lindsey among them, which holds that the literal city of Babylon is to be rebuilt in the last days, so God can destroy her.

There are also some who teach that the "Babylon" mentioned in chapter 17, is not the same entity as the "Babylon" mentioned in chapter 18. They maintain that the whore of chapter 17 represents "ecclesiastical Babylon," by which they usually mean, the Roman Catholic Church; and that the entity described in chapter 18 is "commercial Babylon," or, the world economic system.

I don't agree with any of them. I've explained at some length why I believe Babylon represents the entire corrupt world system, religious, educational, cultural, and economic, which Anti-Christ uses to ascend to power, and then, once he's in power, casts them aside, and rules by raw military might. I suggested that's what we're seeing today; and that once the liberals and atheists are firmly established in power, they intend to scrap the Constitution, and the United Nations charter, and all other vestiges of freedom and democracy, and rule by naked brute force - until Jesus comes back and destroys them, and assumes the power and dominion over the earth, which is rightfully His - and you won't hear anything like that being preached in the liberal churches, or taught in the public schools.

At any rate, I want to take it up there, and plunge into chapter 18. "And after these things I saw another angel come down from heaven, having great power; and the earth was lightened with his glory." Chapter 17 announces the impending destruction of Babylon;

chapter 18 sets out a description of this judgment, and of her actual destruction. The chapter may be divided into five topics: (1) An angel proclaims the fall of Babylon - vs 1-2, and enumerates the reasons for her fall - vs.3; (2) The angel warns God's people to come out of her, vs. 4-5, and to assist in her destruction, vs. 6-8; (3) There is great lamentation over her fall by those who have participated in her sinful pleasures, and shared in her profits, vs. 9-19; it specifically mentions the kings, vs. 9-10; the merchants, vs. 11-17, and the ship-masters and seamen, vs. 17-19 (4) God's people are called upon to rejoice over her fall, vs. 20; and (5) the final destruction of the city is described, vs. 21-24.

I will say that, once we've finished this chapter, we'll be closing in on the end of the book - after 5 years of study - we started the first Wednesday night in January, 2007. And after this chapter, then the next chapter, chapter 19, describes the battle of Armageddon; chapter 20 describes the final judgment; and chapters 21-22 describe heaven. I've been asked, "When are you going to talk about, 'Whosoever will?' You've said a lot about predestination and election - what about 'Whosoever will?'"

The answer is, that language occurs in Chapter 22, verse 17 - four verses before the end of the book. I've simply been taking the book one verse at a time - and the reason I haven't talked about free will yet, is because John hasn't mentioned it, in the material we've been going over. If you think John should have brought it up sooner than that, your quarrel is with him, not me. I'm simply discussing the material as we come to it. And if this study has shown me nothing else, it shows how much of the material we ignore, and how we pick and choose the verses which we like.

Bro. Charles talked Sunday night about how folks are inclined to ignore the Old Testament, and only preach from the New Testament. We've not been picking and choosing which verses we want to talk about. We've discussed every single one, the difficult passages as well as the easy passages; and tonight's text falls into the former category - it's one of the more difficult passages in Revelation, or in the entire Bible, for that matter.

I said as we closed last week, that I've never heard anyone preach a sermon from chapter 18 of Revelation - except the five times I've preached through the book of Revelation; and I covered this chapter in some fashion, of course. I'm not sure I did a particularly good job, because each time, I covered chapter 18 in one week - I devoted about 20 minutes to it - which is less than a minute a verse, since it has 24 verses. Given the fact that I'm 66 years old, and the fact that our enemies are making a big effort to close down all Bible believing churches, I may never preach on it again - so this time, I'm going to try and give it a bit more attention than that.

Let me say, first of all, that there are several other passages in the Bible - all of them in the Old Testament - which have language similar to what we read here. This chapter talks about the fall of Babylon - in Isaiah 14, beginning at vs. 12, we read about the fall of Lucifer. There is a dirge, a song bewailing the doom of Babylon, in Isaiah 13, vs. 19-22, and another in Jeremiah, chapter 50, beginning with verse 39, and continuing on through chapter 51. The book only has 52 chapters, so it's right near the end of the book.

There is a dirge about the destruction of Tyre, in Ezekiel 27: 1-11; a dirge about the destruction of Edom in Isaiah 34: 11-15; and a dirge about the destruction of Ninevah in Zepheniah 2: 13-15. These all contain language very similar, or even identical, to the language set out in chapter 18 of Revelation; as you can see, if you read them when you get home.

So, the first thing John says is that: "I saw another angel come down from heaven." This is not the same angel who's just showed him the woman sitting on the scarlet colored best, and explained to him what that means. That's the general pattern in the book of Revelation; for each new revelation, each new announcement, God sends another, different angel. For example, in chapter 14, in verse 6, he sees "another angel", the first angel who's mentioned in that particular chapter; then in verse 8, "there followed another angel"; then in verse 9 "the third angel followed them, saying. . . ."

Then, in verse 15, "another angel came out of the temple, saying;" then in verse 17 "another angel came out of the temple;" then in verse 19, "another angel came out of the altar." So that's what's happening here - God has another communication to make, and so He sends "another angel."

The announcement, of course, concerns the fall of Babylon, and God's intention, His determination, to destroy her. Compare this to chapter 10 of Revelation, verse 5 and following, where a "mighty angel" comes down from heaven, plants one foot on the land, one foot on the sea, and announces: "that there should be time no longer." That is, he announces God's intention to retake possession of the earth. Here, we have a similar angel with a similar message; he announces Gods intention to destroy Babylon.

It describes the angel as "having great power." Now, let me show you something. We've just read chapter 10, verse 1, which spoke about "a mighty angel" coming down from heaven. This angel, in our text, is said to "have great power." You'd say, "OK, it means pretty much the same thing, doesn't it?" A "mighty angel," and one who has "great power?" In English, the difference is not readily apparent, although the King James translators have done the best they could to show a distinction, by translating one as "power" and one as "might."

But the meaning is different. In chapter 10, vs. 1, the "mighty angel" is said to be "physically strong"; the same Greek word, *ischuros',* is used, for example, to describe a strong wind, or a strong earthquake. The word translated "powerful" here, is *exousia,* which means, authority. The type of power a king might have, for example. It's the same word Jesus uses in Matthew 28, where he tells the disciples, "All power is given unto me in heaven and in earth." It means, not physical strength, but the power of authority.

I bring up that point of grammar to show that the Bible is carefully written, and that the original Greek captures shades of meaning that our English Bible misses. My point is that God inspired the exact words He wanted John to write - and those who do not believe in plenary verbal, word by word, inspiration, are not serious Bible students, and are misleading folks. Those who claim that the message is inspired, but the words are not, are not interested so much in what
God has to say, as what they can make it say, how they can twist the meaning to suit their own ideas.

So it describes the angel as having "great authority." The Bible clearly indicates that there are different ranks of angels - think of the term "archangel" - and so the meaning could be that he has authority over other angels. We've seen numerous angels all through the book; but the importance of this message it shown by the fact that a higher ranking angel is sent to deliver it. The other way of looking at it is this: who gave him the authority? God, of course. He is sent to announce the defeat of the beast, Anti-Christ who, we're told in Rev. 13: 2, was given "great authority" by "the dragon," meaning Satan.

So the real battle is not between the angel and Anti-Christ, but between God and Satan. John is contrasting the authority given Anti-Christ with the authority given to the angel.

Then it says that: "the earth was lightened with his glory." Light is, everywhere in the Bible, associated with the presence of God. For example, this is the Christmas season; and we read in the Christmas story, in Luke 2:8-9 "And there were in the same country, shepherds abiding in the field, keeping watch over their flocks by night. and lo, the angel of the Lord came upon them, and the glory of the Lord shown round about them."

Paul, in describing his conversion experience to King Agrippa, recounted, Acts 26:13 - "At midday, O King, I saw in the way a light from heaven, above the brightness of the sun, shining round about me and them which were with me."

When they had imprisoned Peter, and the angel came to deliver him from the prison, it says, "And, behold, the angel of the Lord came upon him, and a light shined in the prison." In the book of Habakkuk, we're familiar with the words written in Hab. 3:2, where he prays "O, Lord, revive thy work in the midst of the years." And in the next verse, verse 3, he goes on to describe God as follows: "God came from Teman, and the Holy One from mount Paran. Selah. His glory covered the heavens, and the earth was full of his praise. And his brightness was as the light."

When we get to chapter 21 of Revelation, John's vision of heaven, we read, in verse 23: "And the city had no need of the sun, neither of the moon, to shine in it: for the glory of God did lighten it, and the Lamb is the light thereof." We similarly read, in Ezek. 43:2 - "And behold, the glory of the God of Israel came from the way of the east: and his voice was like a noise of many waters; and the earth shined with his glory."

And finally, in the prophecy of Isaiah, chapter 60 verse 1 - he's already predicted the fall of Babylon - in Chapter 21, verse 9, he says "Babylon is fallen, is fallen" - and now in chapter 60, he says that when that occurs: "Arise, shine, for thy light is come, and the glory of the Lord is risen upon thee. For, behold, the darkness shall cover the earth, and gross darkness the people: but the Lord shall arise upon thee, and his glory shall be seen upon thee."

So it's clear that the glory of God is often, and consistently, compared to light; and it's equally clear that the earth is pictured as being in darkness. Dr. A. T. Robertson comments: "So recently has the angel come from the Presence of God that in passing he flings a broad belt of light across the dark earth." Another commentator notes, we're told in Exodus that, after Moses had been on the mountain receiving the Ten Commandments - those Ten Commandments which it is now illegal to display in public schools - and after Moses came back down the mountain, his face shone with the glory of God, after he had been in God's presence. Just so, the earth was illuminated by the splendor which comes from the glory of God, when the angel had been in God's presence. And the original language here, reinforces this point. Where the King James language reads, "The earth was lightened with his glory", a more exact reading would be, "the earth was lightened by reason of his glory."

Yet another commentator, Jacob Seiss, whom I've quoted before, because he writes much better stuff than I can, he says: "The garment of Jehovah is light and such intense luminousness everywhere attaches to what is divine, whilst the enlightening of things by the glory of God and the Lamb is specially spoken of in these visions."

So the angel had light, enlightenment, which enabled him to discern the truth of his own predictions, and also to inform and enlighten the world about the coming events; and he also had the power, the authority, to accomplish the judgment predicted.

It is true, of course, that all ministers, and all Christians, have the light of God, since Jesus said, in the Sermon on the Mount, "Ye are the light of the world." And we are commanded to diffuse that light to those who are still in darkness, because Jesus added, "Let your light so shine before men that they may see your good works, and glorify your Father which is in heaven."

So this is a chapter about judgment. In Revelation 16:19, we read that, when this happens: "Great Babylon came in remembrance before God." Note the words, "before God." Her judgment did not occur on earth, but in heaven; but the sentence was executed on earth. Just as in our criminal justice system; they pronounce sentence at the courthouse, but the sentence is carried out, later, at the state penitentiary. So, although sentence has already been pronounced by God in heaven, in chapter 16, it is not until chapter 18, the chapter we're now embarking upon, that we see the sentence executed, on earth.

The passages we've just read not only picture the earth as being in darkness, but they also show that, as the end of the age approaches, that darkness will increase. Hear again what Isaiah says. Speaking of the last days, he prophesies: "For behold, darkness shall cover the earth, and gross darkness the people." So, when the angel descends, the earth is full of moral darkness. The illumination of the earth by his glory presages the destruction of darkness and the introduction of light, which will be the overthrow of Babylon, and the introduction of the Millennial Kingdom.

Now, where do we stand today? Look around you - is the world getting better and better, as the post-millennialists teach; or is it dark, and getting darker? Today is the 70th anniversary of Pearl Harbor - for those who were alive then, it was like 9/11 - they could all tell you where they were, and what they were doing, when they first heard the news - it was early on a Sunday afternoon, in this part of the country.

The next day, Pres. Roosevelt went before a joint session of Congress and asked for a declaration of war. He said, near the end of his speech: "With confidence in our armed forces, with the unbounding determination of our people, we will gain the inevitable triumph - so help us God." Reckon you could read that speech in a public school today? Reckon you could post that speech on the wall of a courthouse today? They made us take down a copy of President Lincoln's speech off the wall of the Pulaski County courthouse, down in Someset, Kentucky, because it contained a religious reference.

Is the world getting better, or is it getting worse? Most of you are about my age. Did you ever think you'd see sodomy legalized? Did you ever think the public schools would be teaching impressionable kids all about sodomy? Did you ever think the Moslems would be a threat to the United States? Did you ever think abortion would be legal? And, behind it all, the ever present threat of nuclear annihilation. For the first time in the history of the race, we have the ability to destroy ourselves, and to destroy the planet. And we've become so accustomed to living with the nuclear threat, that no one pays much attention to it.

In 1940, just after the Germans had conquered France, British Prime Minister Winston Churchill made a speech to Parliament, urging them to continue the war. One thing he said was, if Hitler wins the war, "then the whole world, including the United States, including all that we have known and cared for, will sink into the abyss of a new Dark Age made more sinister, and perhaps more protracted, by the light of perverted science." That was more than 71 years ago; and today the world seems to be on the brink of just such an age of darkness. So I think this text from Revelation is quite timely; and that we are living in the last days John was describing.

And what the angel says is, look at verse 2: "And he cried mightily with a strong voice, saying, Babylon the great is fallen, is fallen, and is become the habitation of devils, and the hold of every foul spirit, and a cage of every unclean and hateful bird." We've encountered this language before in the book of Revelation. In chapter 14, vs. 8, we read: "And there followed another angel, saying, Babylon is fallen, is fallen, that great city, because she made all nations drink of the wine of the wrath of her fornication."

Both these verses are quoting what Isaiah had said, 900 years before - Isa. 21:9: "And, behold, here cometh a chariot of man, with a couple of horsemen. And he answered and said, Babylon is fallen, is fallen; and all the graven images of their gods, he hath broken unto the ground."

At the time Isaiah uttered this prophecy, Babylon wasn't a place of any particular importance; so he was predicting what was going to happen, nearly 300 years later. The fact that the phrase - actually, in Greek, it's just one word, *epesen* - but it's repeated two times, and that's for emphasis, and to show the certainty of its fulfillment.

You'll also note that it's in the past tense - in Greek, it's the second aorist active indicative, if you're interested - but John's meaning is: "Babylon has already fallen" - although, of course, it hadn't actually occurred at the time John was writing, and hasn't occurred yet. But the event is so inevitable, so immutably fixed in the counsels of God, that it is spoken of as having already occurred. Dr, A.T. Robertson calls this language, "A solemn dirge of the damned."

Well, there I think I'm going to leave it for tonight. We didn't get very far - we only covered one verse. The chapter has 24 verses; so if we continue at that rate, it will be come time in June of next year before we get through the chapter. Maybe we'll pick up speed as we go along.

I will, in closing, repeat what I've said before. In 60 years of hearing Baptist preaching, I've never heard a single sermon on this chapter. We may not be here for another sixty years, waiting for the preachers to get around to it. That means that, if you miss our study here on Wednesday night, you'll probably never get another chance to hear this text explained. So it's important that you be here next Wednesday, and every Wednesday, as we continue our study of Revelation 18.

Rev. 18:1-8

Tonight we return to the 18th chapter of Revelation. You'll recall that we began our study of this chapter last Wednesday night. I told you that this chapter and the previous chapter, chapter 17, form part of the same prophecy – there were no chapter divisions in the original, of course. Chapter 17 announces the impending destruction of Babylon, and chapter 18 describes that judgment.

I also told you the chapter may be divided into 5 parts: (1) An angel announces the fall of Babylon, and gives the reasons for her fall, vs. 1-3; (2) The angel warns God's people to come out of her, and to assist in her destruction. Vs. 4-8; (3) There is great lamentation over her by those who have participated in her sinful pleasures and shared in her profits, vs. 9-19. This is the longest section of the chapter, and it specifically mentions kings, merchants, and seamen; (4) God's people are called upon to rejoice over her fall, vs. 20; and (5) the final destruction of the city is described, vs. 21-24.

We compared the dirge over Babylon to several passages in the Old Testament which are similar, and describe the fall of Babylon, or of Lucifer, or of Tyre, or of Ninevah, or of Edom. Verse 1 describes the angel as having "great power." Of course, God is the one Who gave him this power; and we've already seen that Satan is the one who gave AntiChrist his power. So what we have is a contest between the power of God and the power of Satan. Such a struggle has been going on ever since the garden of Eden, and continues today; but this chapter describes the culmination, the final wind-up of this age-long struggle.

And it says that we're going to win – and that was a message that God's persecuted people in John's day needed to hear; and it's a message that needs to be proclaimed today – there's a war going on, and we're on the winning side. And you won't hear that preached in many churches today.

Then we noted that it says when the angel came down: "the earth was lightened with his glory." We looked at other places in the Bible where God is compared to light, and we also noted that the verse necessarily implies that the world was lying in darkness. I read you a part of one of Winston Churchill's speeches warning about "a new dark age, made more sinister and more protracted, by the lights of perverted science." I also noted last Wednesday night, that it was Pearl Harbor Day, and read you a part of Pres. Roosevelt's speech on that occasion, promising that "we will gain the inevitable triumph – so help us God."

And I speculated whether you could read Pres. Roosevelt's speech today in a public school, or post it on a courthouse wall; and noted that the Kentucky Atheists Association had filed suit to make them take down one of Pres. Lincoln's speeches that contained similar language. My conclusion was that the "new dark age" Churchill had feared, seems to be fast approaching. Anyhow, that was last week.

Now today, before we plunge into the latter half of verse 2, which is where we were when we stopped last week, look back at the beginning of the verse: "And he" - that is, the angel - "and he cried mightily with a strong voice saying, Babylon is fallen, is fallen." The Greek word translated "mightily" - *ischui* - implies that he cried "with all his might." Matthew Henry thinks that the meaning is, he announced the coming destruction so loudly "that all might hear the cry, and might see how well this angel was pleased to be the messenger of such tidings."

He also suggests that the repetition of the words - "Babylon the great is fallen, is fallen," indicates "a double fall." First, she falls into apostasy, into wickedness; and then she falls into ruin, because God judges her for her wickedness. We, of course, believe that is always the case; that when an individual, or a nation, or a society, falls into wickedness, it won't be long before they fall into ruin before the judgment of God. If so, then America's in trouble.

But then, look at the remainder of the verse: "Babylon the great is fallen, is fallen, and is become the habitation of devils, and the hold of every foul spirit, and a cage of every unclean and hateful bird." He's painting a picture of desolation, of course; of a town or city that used to have people there, but is now abandoned. Not long after June and I married - I believe it was in August of 1973 - we took a week's vacation and drove around the back roads of Colorado and Utah.

And I remember going through one, what they called a "ghost town" - there had been a silver mine there, a hundred years ago, and when the mine played out, the town died, was abandoned, and now there was nothing there except the buildings. There are numerous such ghost towns in that part of the United States. That's the kind of thing John's talking about.

There are numerous passages in the Old Testament where Isaiah, and Jeremiah, and Zepheniah, predict such a future for Babylon, or, in Zepheniah's case, for Ninevah - which were the great cities of that day. For example, in Jer. 50: 39, he says, concerning Babylon: "Therefore the wild beasts of the desert with the wild beasts of the islands shall dwell there, and the owls shall dwell therein: and it shall be no more inhabited for ever; neither shall it be dwelt in from generation to generation."

Then, in the following chapter, Jer 51:37, still talking about Babylon, he says: "And Babylon shall become heaps, a dwellingplace for dragons, an astonishment, and an hissing without an inhabitant." And there are a number of similar passages - I'll not take the time to read them all. Isa. 13:21. 14:23; 21:9; 34:8-15; Jer. 9:11; Zeph. 2:14. So John is here predicting a similar doom for the world system, which he represents as a city.

The city is described as becoming three things: it says Babylon will be "the habitation of devils." The word is *daimonion,* meaning "demon," rather than Satan himself - we've talked about "demons" before, and I'll not repeat what I said then. But it's said to be the "habitation" of devils, or demons. The Greek word used here - *katoiketerion* - occurs only one other time in the New Testament, in Eph. 2:22, where believers are said to be the "habitation" of the Holy Spirit.

As I've said frequently, Greek has shades of meaning that are lost in the English translation, and the word used here carries the meaning of a place where one settles down with the intention of staying there permanently. And before you rush out and buy one of the new translations, that's supposed to make it so much clearer, in this instance, they don't. The American Standard Version uses the same word as the King James Version, "habitation." The Revised Standard Version, the New American Standard, and the New King James Version, all use the word "dwellingplace." Now, I ask you, is the word "dwellingplace" a whole lot different from the KJV word, "habitation?"

The New Living Bible, which is always further off base than any of the others, uses the term "hideout," and the New International Version uses the word "home." Again, I ask, is there really any difference between the words "habitation" and "home?" But the idea is, that the demons have moved in to stay, and they aren't fixing to leave.

The city is also called "the hold of every foul spirit." The word translated "foul" - *akathartos* - is the word which, in the Old Testament, signified something that was ceremonially unclean. So the spirit of this present age, the spirit of the world, is said to be characteristically impure. Babylon is said to be the "hold" of such impure spirits. The word translated "hold" - *phylake* - is the same word that is also translated "cage" in the next phrase, "a cage of every unclean and hateful bird."

It comes from a verb - *phulasso* - which means, "to guard." John well knew what a "guard" was, because there was one watching him write the letter, to make sure he didn't go anywhere. The word can be used to mean a prison, or it can mean a "guardhouse," the place where the guards would stay; in Habakkuk 2:1, the word is used to describe a watch-tower.

And here, I think, is the meaning. Babylon, the city pictured, had in its heyday had troops, soldiers, guarding the walls of the city, to assure that everything and everyone, was safe. Now the only guards it has are evil spirits. It's also called "a cage of every unclean and hateful bird." The word translated "bird" here, *orneon* - occurs only 3 times in the New Testament; the other two occurrences are in Rev. 19:17, and Rev. 19:21 - it's not the usual word for "bird." And the other two times it's used, in chapter 19, it's speaking of vultures.

So, what's he saying? The picture he's describing is one of a house, or a fort, or a city, in ruins. It's a picture of complete destruction; a city sacked and ruined, never to be rebuilt - as the once great city of Babylon had now become; a picture of utter desolation.

Bullinger says that the world system "is to be destroyed as utterly as was Babylon of old, and will become as odious, and loathsome, and detestable as the literal Babylon, the abode of monsters is." A.T. Robertson describes it this way: "The evil spirits, watching over the fallen city like night birds, that wait for their prey, build their eyeries in the broken towers which rise from the ashes of the city."

So what John's saying is, that the world's like a bird cage, that's got a lot of impure and detestable birds in it. This present world system is like a bird cage. America's like a bird cage. Washington, D.C.'s like a bird cage; and it's got a lot of birds in it that God considers impure, and whom He detests. Want me to name some of them?

How about the crowd in Washington, D.C.? Did you notice, on the news, Obama went to church last Sunday? December - and it's the first time since Easter that he's been there. How about the crowd that run the abortion clinics? How about the crowd that operate the riverboat? How about the public schools who have ball games and band contests on Sunday, and keep kids out of church? How about the liberal churches and seminaries? America's like a bird cage, and it's got a lot of "unclean and hateful birds" in it.

Today, of course, their evil influence is offset, to at least some extent, by born-again Christians, who live separated lives, and by soul-winning churches that get the gospel out. But after the church is raptured out - which is the time John's talking about here - there aren't going to be any Christians, or any churches. All that will be left are a bunch of demons, and evil spirits guarding a cage full of liberal preachers, and secular humanists, and the American Atheist Association, and the United States Supreme Court - and all the other "unclean and hateful birds," with which our country abounds.

Thus, John is saying that, as a cage is full of birds, so will Babylon be full of evil spirits and demons, controlling the great apostasy of the last days. Now, look at vs 3: "For all nations have drunk of the wine of the wrath of her fornication, and the kings of the earth have committed fornication with her, and the merchants of the earth are waxed rich through the abundance of her delicacies."

Verses 1 and 2 announce the fact of Babylon's impending destruction; and in verse 3, the angel tells us the reason God is going to destroy the world system. Now, of course, God doesn't owe any of us an explanation for what He does, or why He does it; but, in this case, perhaps because of the great destruction intended - it is the destruction of the entire world system - He does reveal why He is fixing to destroy the entire world order.

So, what's the reason? What does this verse tell us? The most obvious fact is, perhaps, that God is opposed to the liquor business - He speaks of "the wine of the wrath of her fornication"; and that God opposes sexual immorality - the word "fornication" occurs twice - and so we can assume that drunkenness and sexual immorality played some role in the sinful practices of Babylon.

But this is primarily meant as symbolic language, of course, She is said to have committed spiritual fornication, and to have led the nations of the world to do so. She sinned herself, and she led others to sin. In other words, she had beguiled and corrupted the nations of the earth, leading them into estrangement from God, and into pollution and sin. By "adultery," he means spiritual adultery; in other words, Babylon had been the means of seducing men from God and leading them into sinful practices.

Matthew Henry phrases it this way: "The wickedness of Babylon had been very great, for she had not only forsaken the true God herself, and set up idols, but had with great art and industry drawn all sorts of men into the spiritual adultery, and by her wealth and luxury had retained them in her interest."

Babylon is also being punished because "the merchants of the earth are waxed rich through the abundance of her delicacies." The word translated delicacies, *stranos.* occurs only here in the New Testament, and has more punch to it than the English translation suggests. It means "excessive luxury"; it means "arrogant luxury"; one translator suggests "insolent luxury" or "wantonness." What is condemned here is excessive luxury; the rich get richer, while the poor get poorer.

Jamieson, Faussett and Brown say that: "The reference is not to earthly merchandise, but to spiritual wares, indulgences, idolatries, superstitions, worldly compromises, wherewith the harlot, that is, the apostate church, has made merchandise of men." So the general meaning is that, in the last days, society will turn away from God, and instead seek above all money, pleasure, luxury. And I think there is no doubt we are living in just such a time today.

But who does it say was responsible for leading the people of the earth astray? One group it identifies is "the kings." The Greek word is *basileus*; and it doesn't only mean a "king", in the sense of being a hereditary monarch - like the king or queen of England, for example - but it has a broader implication; Thayer's lexicon says it can mean "a leader of the people; a lord; a commander; the lord of the land."

In our country, of course, and in most countries today, they don't have kings; many have, or at least pretend to have, democratically elected governments. That doesn't change the sense of the text; the meaning is, that in the last days, men will turn away from God, and the government will encourage them to do so. The governments will no longer hold, or recognize, religious values. Isn't that what we're seeing today?

Yes, we are, in many ways. You know that I think the godless men who run our government are using the public education system to make atheists out of the next generation of young people. 40 years ago, the schools wouldn't have had activities during church time on Sunday morning. We can tick off the list of things the government's done within our own lifetimes, to destroy religious values. Abortion on demand; state operated lotteries - fifty years ago, lotteries were illegal in all 50 of the states. - now, 48 of the 50 states have state sponsored lotteries. The legalized sale of alcohol, which I continue to oppose - I think Billy Sunday and Mordechai Ham were right, when they called the liquor industry "demon rum."

Kentucky inaugurated a governor yesterday - Gov. Steve Beshear was returned to office for a second four-year term, and they swore him in yesterday. He was a Presbyterian minister's son, in Dawson Springs, Kentucky - and in the four years he's been in office, he's done everything in his power to promote the gambling interests in Kentucky. The list goes on and on - I think it's clear that the government is in revolt against God, and against traditional values, and is doing its utmost to lead men away from God.

John's words here, echo what Jeremiah said in chapter 51 of his prophecy, and verse 7: "Babylon hath been a golden cup in the

Lord's hand, that made all the earth drunken: the nations have drunken of her wine; therefore the nations are mad." And if ever we lived in a world gone mad, that time is certainly today.

But I want to go on, and see if we can cover a little more tonight, before the time's gone. "And I heard another voice from heaven, saying, Come out of her, my people, that ye be not partakers of her sins, and that ye receive not of her plagues." I told you at the beginning of the chapter, that it has five divisions. The first three verses, which we've just read, announce the impending destruction of Babylon, the world system, and give us the reason therefor. The next five verses, verses 4-8, warn God's people to come out of Babylon.

I've mentioned this theme before; and the reason I keep coming back to it, is because John keeps coming back to it. God has always called for separation from the world, and Christianity is largely a religion of leaving things. In Genesis 12, God called Abraham to get out of his country, and from his kindred, and God said, "Go to a land that I will shew thee." And, the author of Hebrews tells us, having been so commanded, Abraham went out, even though he didn't know where he was headed.

A few chapters further on, we see Lot being told to get out of Sodom before God destroyed the city. Separation was a theme of the Old Testament prophets: Isaiah 48:20 - "Go ye forth of Babylon, flee ye from the Chaldeans, with a voice of singing."

Jeremiah 51:6 - "Flee out of the midst of Babylon, and deliver every man his soul, be not cut off in her iniquity." Jeremiah 51:45 - "My people, go ye out of the midst of her, and deliver ye every man his soul from the fierce anger of the Lord."

In the New Testament, we have a similar emphasis. II Cor. 6:17 - "Wherefore, come out from among them, and be ye separate, saith the Lord."

A Roman Catholic writer, and monk, who lived about the year 1500, shortly before the time of Martin Luther, and thought, like Luther, that the Catholic Church needed reform, wrote these lines - in Latin, they rhyme - but the English translation is: "Ye who desire to live a godly life, depart; for, although all things are lawful in Rome, yet to be godly is unlawful."

Does that sound like today in America? You can do anything, except live a godly life? You can say anything, except talk about

Jesus Christ? As I've said before, churches generally used to call for living a separated, godly life; and fundamentalist churches, especially, did - it was one of our distinctives, something which set us apart from other churches and groups - fundamentalists didn't do certain things; fundamentalist parents didn't let their kids do certain things. But we've lost that, today. You rarely hear a preacher calling for Christian separation.

Why? Has the Bible changed? The reason, of course, is because most churches have gotten so desperate to draw a crowd, that they don't want to say anything to upset anybody.

Someone says, "Wait a minute. Who's John talking to? Who's supposed to come out of Babylon? I thought the church had been raptured out almost 7 years before this." The answer is, that some people will be saved during the tribulation; there will be saved people on earth, Israel will be on the earth - and to those who believe and follow Jesus Christ, the angel's message is, "Come out of her, my people."

Come out, for two reasons: (1) so you won't be partaking of her sins; and (2) so you won't suffer when God judges her. I've got more to say along that line, and I can't get through it tonight; so we'll have to take it up again there next week. It'll be the week before Christmas, and lots of folks will be tempted to skip church for holiday activities. We'll still be having church, just the same, and continuing our study in Revelation; and I hope you'll come back next Wednesday.

Rev. 18:1-8

Tonight we return to the 18th chapter of Revelation. As we've seen already, chapters 17 and 18 form part of the same prophecy. There were no chapter divisions in the original. They were added by later editors, to make it easier to locate any particular passage. But chapters 17 and 18 constitute parts of a connected whole. Chapter 17 announces the impeding destruction of Babylon, and chapter 18 describes her actual destruction.

The chapter before us, chapter 18, may be divided into five sections: (1) An angel announces the fall of Babylon, and gives the reasons for her fall, vs. 1-3; (2) The angel warns God's people to come out of her, and to assist in her destruction, vs. 4-8 ; (3) There is great lamentation over her by those who have participated in her sinful pleasures, and shared in her profits, vs. 9-19, which is the longest section of the chapter. And most Bible students, when they think of Revelation 18, think of this section, and the words, "Alas, Babylon!"; the phrase occurs three times. (4) God's people are called upon to rejoice over her fall, verse 20; and (5) the final destruction of the city is described, vs. 21-24.

Last week, we looked at the phrase "Babylon is fallen, is fallen," in verse 2, and noted that the words are repeated twice, not only for emphasis, but because Babylon, which represents the world system, is going to fall in two ways. First, she falls into apostasy, into wickedness; and then she falls into ruin, because God judges her. And I commented that America seems to be headed in that direction, with alarming speed.

And I commented that the last part of verse 2, about Babylon having become the habitation of evil spirits, and of buzzards, which is what kind of birds it's talking about, shows that it's become a ghost town - and I talked about ghost towns in the Rocky Mountains. And we read some passages from the Old Testament, Specifically, from Isaiah and Jeremiah, that predicted the same thing.

It describes Babylon as having become "the habitation of devils"; and I showed you where some of the new versions say, "the home of devils', and asked whether it's worth trashing the King James and putting out a new version on the assumption that people will know what a "home" is, but will have no clue what a "habitation" is. You should reject the new versions, if for no other reason, because they insult your intelligence, and imply that we're all too dumb to read the English language.

Verse 2 also says Babylon has become "a cage of every unclean and hateful bird." And I opined that America has become a bird cage, that Washington, D.C., is a bird cage, that the public schools and the liberal churches, are bird cages; and we named some of the "unclean and hateful birds" that hold forth there. And I'll bet you won't hear that kind of preaching in any other church in town. Seriously, when was the last time you heard any of the prosperity gospel crowd preach on Revelation 18? Is that chapter not in their

Bibles? Or are they purposely avoiding it, because they don't want to risk making anybody mad?

Anyhow, that was last week. Now, today, we'll take it up there. We had finished discussing the first section of the chapter, verses 1-3, where the angel announces Babylon's fall, and tells us why she's being judged. In the second section, verses 4-8, God warns His people to come out of her, and also urges them to assist in her destruction. We'd just started explaining that part; I'd said that you don't hear much preaching on Christian separation in churches today, not even in fundamental churches.

So I want to take it up there; look at verses 4-5 again: "And I heard another voice from heaven, saying, Come out of her, my people, that ye be not partakers of her sins, and that ye receive not of her plagues. For her sins have reached unto heaven, and God hath remembered her iniquities." Dr. Clarke says that these verses mark a point where God's long-suffering gives place to His justice. Babylon's sins, he notes, "are become so great and enormous that the long-suffering of God must give place to His justice."

These verses, verses 4-5, say 4 things, basically: (1) that God has a people, even in sinful Babylon; (2) that God wants His people to come out of Babylon; (3) that those who remain in Babylon will participate in her judgment, they'll be judged in some fashion; and (4) that at some point, God's patience has an end, and He come to Babylon, and judges her, and punishes her for her sins.

Taking the points in order, he says, first: "And I heard another voice from heaven, saying, Come our of her, my people." I spoke briefly last week about the fact that God has always called his people to separation from the world. We talked about Abraham leaving Ur of the Chaldees, and going to Canaan; and we talked about God telling Lot to leave Sodom. I came across this language in another commentary - this was written by an English commentator, in 1990 - not everything I read you is 200 years old - there are actually some people writing today who believe the Bible and take what it says literally - although I'll concede that they're few and far between. Anyhow, he says: "Just as Lot fled from Sodom before its destruction; the Israelites fled from Egypt; God's people fled Babylon; and the early church fled Jerusalem to avoid persecution before her destruction, so God's people are told to leave Babylon before her destruction comes upon her."

As I explained last week, we understand this passage as referring to the great tribulation; the church will already have been raptured out; so it doesn't concern us, directly - God's not talking to the church, because the church is already gone. But there will be folks saved during the tribulation; and, of course, Israel will still be here. And it is to these folks that God - or the angel - we can't be sure which, since it doesn't tell us whether God Himself is speaking from heaven, or whether it's the voice of yet another angel. But, it is to these folks, Jews, and Gentiles who've been saved during the tribulation - that's who he's speaking to - and at least some of them are living in Babylon.

Bullinger observes that one of the groups that's said to be living in Babylon is, the merchants, and supposes that, if there was money to be made, there'd be Jews there, so it was natural that some Israelites would be living in Babylon. My Jewish son-in-lay wouldn't object to that characterization - Gordon's quite proud of his business acumen - and I will admit that he's the only one in my family who's got any money, and he's made it all himself - when he and Aimee married 12 years ago, they were both about as broke as I am.

So Bullinger may have a point. But, besides that primary interpretation, there's also a secondary interpretation - God put it in the Bible for our admonition, as well as just foretelling what's going to happen during the tribulation. And the point for us to see is, that some of God's people are living in Babylon, meaning that they're living in, hopelessly enmeshed in, the world system. Not all Christians are living separated lives.

I was on the radio back in Kentucky, for 32 years. The biggest fight I ever had during that entire time was when I said a Baptist deacon shouldn't own a liquor store - and the deacons at Lebanon Baptist Church went to the radio station, tried to have me thrown off the air, and threatened to sue me - that was long before I even thought of becoming a lawyer.

And J. T. Whitlock, the station manager, said to them, "Look, I'll give you guys equal time. You can come out here next Sunday morning, and go on the air, and say, 'We're the Baptist deacons he's talking about, and we own a liquor store, and here's why we think it's OK. Our church thinks Baptist deacons should sell liquor, and here's why - I'll donate the time to let you respond.' " Well, not surprisingly, they thought it over, and decided not to take him up on it.

But you get my point. Babylon represents the world system, and there are a lot of Christians who are enmeshed in, mixed up in, the world system. To cite one other example, and then I'll move on, the night my daughter Betsey graduated from Nelson County Baptist School, they let me say the closing prayer - they wouldn't let me preach, because they were afraid of what I'd say. So I began my prayer by thanking God "that we've managed to rescue these kids from the atheists who run the public schools."

I didn't think that was out of line, because that's why we ran a Christian school - because we didn't like the public school. But as soon as I'd said "Amen," before I even got out from behind the pulpit, a guy came running up the aisle, and said, "I resent that! How dare you say such a thing? I'll have you know, I'm a member at Bardstown Baptist Church, I'm a good Christian, and I teach at Nelson County High School - there are a lot of Christians who teach there."

Well, I was polite to him; I thought he had a lot of nerve to come into our church and try to tell us what we could and couldn't say to God in prayer; but I was polite to him. But I thought, "Yeah, that's exactly the problem; you and other Christians who are willing to stand up and spout atheism to Christian kids, and help Satan destroy the next generation." I say, there are a lot of Christians who are living in Babylon, and have gotten themselves mixed up in this Satanic world system.

Another thing to note is that, as Matthew Henry points out, "God may have a people even in Babylon, some of who belong to the election of grace." Now, think that through for a minute. If God has a people, folks who can get saved, in Godless Babylon, then it's our duty, our job, to preach the gospel there. C. T. Studd, who founded the World Evangelization Fellowship, had a motto: "Some wish to live within the sound of church or chapel bell; I want to run a rescue shop within a yard of hell."

That means we've got a duty, a responsibility, to preach the gospel, not just in church on Sunday morning, but outside the abortion clinics, and at all the haunts of sin. I've told you before that, while Paul and I were at Temple, the City of Springfield decided to block off the public square in the middle of town, one Saturday night, and hold a street dance. It's something the City had not done before, use the public thoroughfare for a dance hall, so Paul and I, and some of the folks from our church, went down to the square on Saturday night, and preached a sermon against dancing - and I'll add, that we had some folks come over and listen to us, that you couldn't get inside a church.

But afterward the folks at Springfield Baptist - the same folks who then chased us out of town - said to me, "What do you think you're doing. Church is the place to preach - not on the courthouse corner during a dance." The answer to that objection is, that's exactly where we need to be preaching the gospel. And if we limit our presentation of the gospel to the church house on Sunday morning, we're not really doing our job. We've got to be preaching the gospel in Babylon, and challenging Satan on his own turf.

The second thing the verse tells us is, that God wants his people to come out of Babylon. I spoke to that point last week, and won't repeat what I said then. God wants his people to live separated lives. One reason is because, by remaining in Babylon, they are giving their implicit sanction and support to Babylon's activities.

Paul wrote to Timothy, I Tim. 5:22 - "Lay hands suddenly on no man, neither be partaker of other men's sins: keep thyself pure." "It is," says Dr. Barnes, "it is implied here that, by remaining in Babylon they would lend their sanction to its sins by their presence, and would, in all probability, become contaminated by the influence around them. This is an universal truth in regard to iniquity, and hence it is the duty of those who would be pure to come out from the world, and to separate themselves from all the associations of evil."

It says, "that ye be not partakers of her sins," and the word translated "partakers", *sunkoinoneo,* occurs only here, and in two other places in the New Testament, and it means "to become a partner with." So the verse says Christians shouldn't go into partnership with the world. Dr. A. T. Robertson translates it as: "That ye have no fellowship with her sins."

So, one reason God's people are commanded to come out of the world is, to avoid giving the world their stamp of approval. In the Catholic church, a Catholic is not allowed to read a book on religion, the Bible or anything else, unless it has the word *"impramatur,"* and below it, the bishop's name, printed on the title page. It's the bishop's stamp of approval; it means that he considers the book doctrinally sound, and that Catholics may read it. It means, in effect, "I approve of this book."

That's what Christians do when they fellowship with the world; they put their stamp of approval on what the world's doing - and that's what this chapter warns against, and why Jesus commands His followers: "Come out of her, my people."

The other reason why God commands His people to come out of Babylon is, "that ye be receive not of her plagues." The Armenians, the falling from grace crowd, take this as meaning, if you live a worldly life, you'll fall from grace; you'll lose your salvation, and wind up in hell. But you have to read this language in light of everything else the New Testament says on the subject. Paul explained to the Corinthians, I Corinthians 3:15, that if any Christian lived a worldly life instead of a godly life, "he shall suffer loss; but he himself shall be saved; yet so as by fire."

Think of Lot's wife. She made it out of Sodom alive; but she couldn't quite bear to part with all that she'd known and cared about there, and so she looked back. Did she lose her salvation? Not if she were saved, she didn't - but she lost her life.

Another example from the Old Testament is a man named Korah, and his two accomplices, Dothan and Abiram. They spoke against Moses, and against the order of worship that God had commanded, and God determined to destroy them. And before He does, God sends Moses to warn everybody else to get away from Korah and his two friends. Numbers 16:26 - "And he," that is, Moses, "and he spake unto the congregation, saying, Depart, I pray you, from the tents of these wicked men, and touch nothing of theirs, lest ye be consumed in all their sins."

And the people do, they get away from the tents of Korah, Dothan and Abiram; and then God swallows the three of them alive into hell. In a similar manner, God warns those in Babylon to flee, so that they may not be involved in her destruction. And God not only called his people to come out of Babylon, but he calls them effectually.

What does that mean? I've been skirting around this question for five and a half years now; let me address it plainly, meet it head-on. The basic theological position of Southern Baptists, the group by which Paul and I - and John R. Rice, and Lee Robertson, and most founders of the fundamentalist movement - the group where we started out, and by which we were ordained - their basic theological position is set out in a book called ABSTRACT OF SYSTEMATIC THEOLOGY, which was written by James P. Boyce, for use as a textbook at the seminary. This is, in other words, what the men who organized the Southern Baptist Convention, believed.

Chapter 23 of Boyce's book is entitled "Outward and Effectual Calling." It's readily available on line, you can pull it up and read it for yourself. But what he says is, that the Bible uses the word "call" in two different senses. One he denominates, labels, the "outward call" - others have used the term "general call." This is the call which, in Boyce's words, "is made indiscriminately to all men." It's what we do when we get up and preach on Sunday mornings - or at the street dance on Saturday night, or on the mission field, or on the radio. We're extending the call of the gospel to all men indiscriminately. It's what Calvary Bible Ministries is doing when we send out Bibles - we're extending the call of the gospel to all men, indiscriminately.

However, Boyce adds "This offer of the gospel meets of itself with no success." And every minister, every soul-winner, has had that experience - you offer it to them, they're not interested. You put your kids in a Christian school for 12 years, and when they graduate, they go out and live like the devil the rest of their lives.

Their failure to accept it is not due to any deficiency in the gospel. The call of God is rejected, Boyce adds, "not from want of evidence, nor from intellectual doubt, but always because of something sinful, either in the heart or will." So the external call is rejected by men, and there is a second type of call, which he denominates, refers to, as an "effectual call."

This call "is accomplished is the Holy Spirit by whose influences the saved are led to the exercise of repentance and faith." So, of those who hear the external call, the only ones who're going to respond to it are those whose hearts God the Holy Ghost enlightens, and enables them to understand it, and to exercise saving faith. They, and they only, will accept the call, and be saved; and this is what he refers to as the "effectual call."

He cites a great number of Scriptures in support of these statements. One is Matt. 20:16: "For many be called, but few chosen." The first clause, "many are called", refers to the outward call, the preaching of the gospel - lots of people hear the gospel proclaimed. The second clause, "but few are chosen," refers to the effectual call, by which the Holy Ghost enlightens men and enables them to exercise saving faith.

A second passage which he cites is I Cor. 1: 23-24, where Paul says: "But we preach Christ crucified, unto the Jews a stumblingblock, and unto the Greeks foolishness; But unto them which are called, both Jews and Greeks, Christ the power of God, and the wisdom of God." Paul says, I've preached the gospel to everybody I could get to listen to me, but most of them didn't pay any attention, or openly scoffed. "But," he adds, "there were some, 'Them which are called,' they accepted it, and believed - and they're the ones I'm writing this epistle to."

I've cited James P. Boyce's book, because he's one of the ones who founded Southern Baptist Theological Seminary, and who helped organize the Southern Baptist Convention - I've cited his book to show that this is what Southern Baptists - the group Paul and I came out of - this is what they originally believed and stood for, what they used to preach. But the Baptists' adherence to this doctrine goes much further than Boyce and the Seminary and the Southern Baptist Convention.

The first statement of faith issues by English Baptists was what's called the London Confession of Faith of 1689. That was the year in which England first established freedom of religion, and so for the first time, Baptists, and other groups outside the official church, had the right to publish their beliefs - and so the English Baptists got together in London, and issued a statement saying, "This is what we believe; this is what we stand for." And the Tenth Article of their statement of faith is entitled "Of effectual calling," and it says what I've just been telling you. Again, the document is readily available on line, you can read it for yourself.

Spurgeon specifically endorsed the London Confession, printed copies of it, handed them out in his church. The London Baptist Confession of 1689 was, in turn, based on and adopted the language of, the Westminster Confession of 1644, which was drawn up by the English Puritans - the same group who came to this country on the Mayflower.

The Westminster Confession of 1644 was, in turn, based upon John Calvin's work, Institutes of the Christian Religion, which was first published in 1536. The section on "Effectual Calling" is found in Book 4, chapter 24, sections 1-3. Calvin, in turn, cites extensively to works by St. Augustine, written more than a thousand years earlier - in 410 A.D., specifically.

I've gone through this extensive explanation to show you that this is what Baptists, and the church generally, has always believed. You're not used to hearing this sort of preaching in Baptist churches (or any place else) - but it is what Baptists have historically believed and taught - and we say right out front that this is a Baptist church, so when you come to North Harrison Baptist Church, you can expect to hear Baptist doctrine.

Well, the time's gone, so I'll quit. We'll take it up next week at verse 5; and I hope to see you all back here at that time. And I hope you all have a Merry Christmas.

Rev. 18:1-8

Tonight we return to Rev. 18. With tonight's study, we complete an even five years of study on Revelation. I began this study on the first Wednesday in January, 2007 - so we've now been at it for 5 years, and we're still in the first part of Chapter 18. That means we've averaged about 3 months on each chapter; so at that rate, we'll get finished sometime in February or March, 2013 - if the Lord delays His coming that long. The rapture may come before then, so we may not be around in March, 2013.

As I've noted before, the chapter before us, chapter 18, is divided into five sections - it describes five things happening - (1) An angel announces the fall of Babylon, and gives the reasons for her fall , verses 1-3; (2) The angel warns God's people to come out of her, and to assist in her destruction, verses 4-8; (3) There is great lamentation over her by those who have participated in her sinful pleasures, and who have shared in her profits, verses 9-19 , which is the longest section of the chapter. The phrase "Alas, Babylon," is repeated three times; (4) God's people are called upon to rejoice over her fall, verse 20; and (5) The final destruction of the city is described.

We've completed our consideration of the first section, verses 1-3, in which the angel announces the fall of Babylon, and gives the reasons for her fall. We're now considering the second section, verses 4-8, in which "another voice," we're not told whether it's God Himself speaking from heaven, or whether it's an angel speaking, but the voice says, "Come out of her, my people." And we've been speaking of the call to Christian separation. I've said, several times, that it's a theme you don't hear much preaching about in churches, not even Baptist churches, not even Fundamental Baptist churches - it's not a theme that's emphasized in churches today. It used to be a fundamentalist distinctive - it set us apart from the Southern Baptists - we called for living a separate lifestyle, and they didn't - but that no longer seems to be the case, except here at North Harrison Baptist Church - we still try to preach the whole counsel of God, and the Bible has quite a bit to say on the point.

I told you last week that verses 4-5 say four things: (1) that God has people, even in sinful Babylon - and we talked about the importance of witnessing in the haunts of sin, as well as at the church house on Sunday morning; (2) that God wants his people to come out of Babylon - and I think I named some areas in which we ought to practice Christian separation; (3) that those who remain in Babylon will participate in her judgment - and I talked about the angel dragging Lot out of Sodom, so he wouldn't be destroyed along with everybody else; and (4) that, at some point, God's patience has an end. I think I'd managed to cover the first three of these points, and reserved the last, the fact that God's patience runs out at some point, had reserved that for this week, before we tackle verse 6.

So, look with me again at verse 4: " And I heard another voice from heaven, saying, Come out of her, my people, that ye be not partakers of her sins, and that ye receive not of her plagues. For her sins have reached unto heaven, and God hath remembered her iniquities." These verses, as I said last week, mark the point at which God's long-suffering gives place to His justice. There was a popular religious song, back in the 1950's - the title was "He," meaning God - and it purported to set out the various attributes of God - to describe God. The last lines of the song went, "Though it makes Him sad to see the way we live, He'll always say, 'I forgive.'" That was a nice thought, a comforting thought, which is why the song was popular - it seemed to say that you could do anything you wanted, on and on and on - and always get away with it. There wouldn't be any "Payday, Someday," to use Dr. Robert G. Lee's phrase.

The only problem with that philosophy is, it's not so. God's patience does have an end, as the text before us plainly declares. And most churches today are no longer sounding that note of alarm. I drive by the big Southern Baptist Church in Georgetown every time I come up here, and I read their big illuminated sign they've got. The sign tells me a lot about the love of God - but very little about his wrath - I think maybe twice in five and half years, they've put up something that might conceivable be construed as a reference to God's judgment.

Nelson County Baptist Church, where I attended for 18 years, has a smaller sign. They change the message every week - and it tells me a great deal about the love of God. They've had the sign up about ten years, now, and if it's ever had a message that mentioned God's wrath, or warned of His coming judgment, I don't recall seeing it. Now, I'm not picking on those two churches - although when you put your message up on a big lighted sign, I think you're inviting public comment on your message - but I'm not particularly singling them out - I think they're representative of a lot of other churches, of most churches today, that don't have a flashing sign out front, but are proclaiming a message over the pulpit, that is identical to what the signs in Georgetown and in Bardstown, tell me - great emphasis on the love of God, very little mention of his wrath - that, despite the fact that the New Testament has a great deal to say about the wrath of God.

Yet, the Southern Baptists insist that the Bible is their sole guide to faith and practice, and that they're proclaiming the whole counsel of God. Are they? I seriously doubt it; and we're doing men no favor when we allow them to remain in Babylon without warning them that God's going to destroy it.

So, look at verse 5 again - you're not likely to hear it at any other church in town. "For her sins have reached unto heaven, and God hath remembered her iniquities." I've noted before that many the things in this chapter are reminiscent of what we read in Jeremiah, chapters 50 and 51 - which shows that the book is carefully written - it wasn't just something that a 90 year old man threw together at random. Verse 5 echoes what Jeremiah said in chapter 51, verse 9: "We would have healed Babylon, but she is not healed: forsake her, and let us go every one into his own country: for her judgment reacheth unto heaven, and is lifted up even to the skies."

Where it says that "her sins have reached unto heaven," the basic notion conveyed by the Greek words - "reached," is two words in Greek, *akoloutheo* and *kollao,* although it's only one in our English translation - the basic idea is that "her sins were such a heap as to reach even unto heaven." The first mention of Babylon in the Bible is in Genesis 11:4, where it speaks of the tower of Babel. "And they said, Go to, let us build us a city and a tower, whose top may reach unto heaven."

The thought may be that, just as man tried to make a tower of Babel that reached to heaven, so now her sins have piled up to heaven instead. There is, perhaps, a double meaning intended; (1) that her sins make such a big pile, are stacked so high, that they extend into the clouds, out of sight - that there's no end to her sins; and (2) that her sins make such a big stack that it's visible even from heaven, and so it's gotten God's attention. Babylon's sin has become so prominent as to attract the attention of God.

Think, for example, of what God said to Cain, Gen. 4:10 - "For the voice of thy brother's blood crieth unto me from the ground." Cain's having murdered his brother, was such a heinous crime that it had attracted God's attention. The same thing occurs in Gen. 18, vs. 20-21. God says: "Because the cry of Sodom and Gomorrah is great, because their sin is very grievous: I will go down now, and see whether they have done altogether according to the cry of it, which is come unto me." Sodom had been getting worse and worse, until eventually it attracted God's attention, and He decided to come down and do something about it.

Law enforcement in America operates that way. As I mentioned Sunday morning, I grew up in a dry town - no legal sale of alcohol. So we had a bunch of bootleggers selling liquor illegally - everybody knew who they were and what they were doing. But they usually left them alone. Occasionally, the problem would become so bad, their activities would get so blatant, that the state ABC - the Alcohol Beverage Commission - would come in, arrest somebody, fine them a hundred dollars, and let them go back to selling liquor again, with the implied warning, try to be more careful next time.

That's the basic idea here - Babylon's been committing all sorts of sin, and seems to have been getting away with it - until eventually her iniquity comes to the full, and God comes down to do something about it. And when he does, unlike the Kentucky court, God's not going to just fine them a hundred dollars and put them back out on the street to continue in their sinful ways.

The public schools used to operate that way, when I taught in them. Little Johnny cuts up in class, and you'd say, "Johnny, sit down and pay attention." And he'd keep at it, you'd warn him two or three times, and eventually you'd say, "OK, that's enough!", and take little Johnny out in the hall and spank him. I say, that's the way it used to be; today, of course, the schools wouldn't spank him if he burned the building down.

And so it says, last part of verse 5 - "and God hath remembered her iniquities." They thought God had forgotten - they had put God out of their minds, and said, "Those preachers down at the fundamental church, don't know what they're talking about it. Forget them. Forget God. Forget judgment to come. We can do as we please. God's not going to do anything about it."

The folks who run the abortion clinics feel that way - "We've murdered 50 million babies, and nothing's happened - don't worry about God." The folks who run the public schools feel that way - "We've destroyed a whole generation of kids now - and God didn't do anything about it. Don't be concerned about what God thinks." The folks who run Child Protective Services feel that way. "We've pretty well destroyed parental authority in this country; we've produced a bunch of kids who think they can do as they please - and God didn't stop us. Forget what it says in the book of Proverbs."

I'm sure Barak Obama must feel that way. "I spent 20 years supporting Jeremiah Wright, while he made a mockery of the Bible, and proclaimed black liberation theology - and the Christians in America voted for me, anyway. They care more about their welfare checks than they do about right and wrong. God's not going to do anything. I can run roughshod over everybody for another four years."

There were people in King David's day who felt that way. God told them, Psalm 50:21 - "Those things hast thou done, and I kept silence; thou thoughtest that I was altogether such an one as thyself: but I will reprove thee, and set them in order before thine eyes. Now consider this, ye that forget God, lest I tear you in pieces, and there be none to deliver." Heard any preaching like that recently, at the liberal church? Do they tell folks, "If you don't get right with God, He's going to tear you in pieces?" Of course not - they believe in a God of all love, who'll let you get away with anything. You've got to come up here to this church, if you want to hear the truth. We'll tell you what you need to hear, not what you want to hear. We'll tell you what God's Word says, not what the liberals at the seminaries say.

I would be remiss in expounding this verse if I did not also say that, while God will remember Babylon's sins, He will forget ours, if we're saved, and those sins are under the blood of Jesus Christ. Jeremiah wrote, chap 31, verse 34 - "For I will forgive their iniquity, and I will remember their sin no more." And the author of Hebrews twice quotes these words from Jeremiah, and applies them to those who are saved - Heb. 8:12; 10:17.

Back in 1978, Ben Speer wrote a song - maybe I'll sing it for you some time -

> I remember the days when I was bent low, with a burden of sin and strife,
> Then Jesus came in and rescued me and gave me a brand new life;
> Now as I thank Him day after day, for washing my sins away,
> It seems I can almost hear the voice of the blesses Savior say,
>
> What sins are you talking about, I don't remember them any more
> From the book of life they've all been torn out
> I don't remember them any more.

Well, let's go on to the next verse: "Reward her even as she rewarded you, and double unto her double according to her works: in the cup which she hath filled fill to her double. How much she hath glorified herself, and lived deliciously, so much torment and sorrow give her: for she saith in her heart, I sit a queen, and am no widow, and shall see no sorrow."

So the ones to whom the words are addressed - we'll ask who that is, in a moment - but the ones to whom God is speaking, are admonished, not only to come out of Babylon, they're also told to participate in her destruction. That's one reason you don't hear any preaching on this chapter - people don't like what it says. It doesn't fit in with their watered down version of Christianity.

The first question is, exactly who's he talking to? The problem with this text is, of course, that it seems to say we're supposed to get even with our enemies, and that doesn't square with what the Sermon on the Mount says about "That ye resist not evil," turn the other cheek, and so on. That difficulty can be avoided if we assume that God's directing these words to the angel who's going to do the deed, and destroy Babylon.

I say, that's a neat solution to the problem - the only problem is, it says, "Reward her as she rewarded you," and it wasn't the angel whom Babylon had been persecuting - it was God's people. So, for the passage to make any sense, you have to assume he's talking to the saints of God, whom Babylon has been persecuting.

The problem, I say again, is that this passage appears to tell God's people they're supposed to take revenge upon their enemies. It doesn't just say that God's going to do it; it doesn't just say we're supposed to pray for God to destroy them. It appears to go beyond that, and admonish those who are being persecuted to go out and assist in the destruction. "Reward her even as she rewarded you." The Greek word translated "reward," *apodidomi,* has perhaps a bit more kick to it than the English word - it means pay her back.

When I was a kid, the kids didn't dare cuss at school - you'd get in bad trouble. Today, of course, they put cuss words in the text books and force the kids to read them. Back then, you'd get sent to the office for cussing at another kid. So, if someone insulted you, a common reply was, "Same to you, and more of it." That phrase got the point across equally well, but didn't violate the rule against profanity.

That's what the word here means, "Same to you, and more of it." Babylon mistreated you - you go and treat her twice as bad as what she did to you." As I say, it's a problem, that generations of Bible scholars have wrestled with - and many preachers have avoided, by ignoring this chapter - and I don't claim to have all the answers. So if my discussion of the point isn't dispositive, I hope it will at least be helpful, and lead you to study what the Bible says, for yourself, instead of simply pretending it's not even in there, like the liberals do.

This is not the only place in the Bible that we find such language - we find similar language in a number of places - and the liberals ignore them, too. I've already referred to the chapters 50 and 51 of Jeremiah, and noted that John seems to be describing the same events that Jeremiah was talking about. In chapter 50, verse 15, those to whom Jeremiah is speaking are admonished to: "Take vengeance upon her; as she hath done, do unto her." In verse 29 of that came chapter, the listeners are admonished to: "Camp against [Babylon] round about; let none thereof escape; recompence her according to her work; according to all that she hath done, do unto her: for she hath been proud against the Lord, against the Holy One of Israel."

Nor is it only Jeremiah that said such things. In Psalm 137: 8-9, we read, also with reference to Babylon: "O daughter of Babylon, who art to be destroyed; happy shall he be, that rewardeth thee as thou hast served us. Happy shall he be, that taketh and dasheth thy little ones against the stones."

Nor is such language confined to the Old Testament. In Galatians 1:8, for example, we find St. Paul saying, "But though we, or an angel from heaven, preach any other gospel unto you than that which we have preached unto you, let him be accursed." The word "accursed" is a the translation of a Greek word which means "let him be condemned to perdition without any hope of redemption." He uses the same word in I Cor. 16:22. He doesn't say, "Let's all pray that they'll repent and get saved;" he says "Let's pray that God will send them to hell." You won't hear that kind of preaching in many churches - but it's right there in your Bible.

In II Tim. 4:14 - and this is after Paul's already said, verse 6 of the same chapter: "The time of my departure is at hand." I know I'm going out to meet God soon. So, in light of that knowledge, what admonition does he give Timothy, his son in the ministry? Verse 14: "Alexander the coppersmith did me much evil: the Lord reward him according to his works." Does he say, "Let's all pray that Alexander the coppersmith gets saved?" No, he says, I pray the Lord will get even with him for the way he's treated me.

And then, as we saw when we studied the 6th chapter of Revelation, at the beginning of the tribulation, when the angel sounded the fifth trumpet, in verse 9, we see the souls of the martyrs under the altar. Do they pray for the salvation of the men who've killed them? Not at all. Their cry is, verse 10: How long, O Lord, holy and true, dost thou not judge and avenge our blood on them that dwell on the earth?"

I watched the pope say midnight mass, Saturday afternoon - because of the time difference, midnight in Rome is late afternoon here. But he read all these prayers - in Latin, of course - asking for the intercession of the saints and martyrs - "St. Stephen martyr, pray for us." I reply that, the only time in the Bible the martyrs in heaven are described as praying for anybody, in Revelation chapter 6 and verse 10, the martyrs are praying for their destruction, not for their salvation. So the pope may be a bit off base on that point - as he is on most other doctrines.

And then, of course, there is the text before us, Rev. 18:6, where those to whom the angel is speaking, are admonished to "reward her even as she rewarded you, and double unto her double according to her works." So, I ask again, how are we to square that with Jesus's words, in the Sermon on the Mount, that you're to love your enemies, and pray for them?

The time's gone, and I'll have to take it up again next week; but one thing it certainly shows is, that Christians don't have to simply lie down and let the wicked walk on them. I've been told for more than fifty years, "Now, Lloyd, Christians shouldn't get involved in politics." So what's happened is, the church folks have stayed home, and let the atheists run the country. We've used that as an excuse to let them take prayer and Bible reading out of the schools, to legalize sodomy, and gay marriage, to open a casino right down the road, to send welfare workers into our homes to tell Christians how to raise their kids, and encourage kids to report their parents, if they don't let the kid do as he pleases - and on, and on.

The folks he's addressing here aren't just told to pray for God's judgment on their enemies - they're directed to take action, do something about it, stand up against the evil and persecution that's going on. And the folks in the seven churches, who had seen Antipas martyred, and their pastor exiled to Patmos, would certainly have understood what he was saying. Don't just sit and pray for God to destroy Caesar, while he kills some more of you. Do whatever you can, to get rid of evil government, and to promote good, godly, government.

Well, that's it for tonight, and for this, the fifth year of our study. I first read this poem on my last radio broadcast in December, 1965, 47 years ago; and I don't think I've missed a year since then, reciting it at the last service of the year, on the radio, wherever I was ministering or attending. It was written by an English preacher named Simon Browne, in 1720.

And now, my soul, another year of thy short life is past
You cannot long continue here, this next may be thy last.

Awake, my soul, with utmost care, thy true condition learn;
What are thy hopes, how sure, how fair, what is thy great concern?

Behold, another year begins, set out afresh for heaven
Seek pardon for thy former sins, in Christ so freely given;

Devoutly yield thyself to God, and on His grace depend;
with zeal pursue the heavenly road, nor doubt a happy end.

Rev. 18:1-8

Tonight we return to the 18th chapter of Revelation. You'll recall that I've told you chapters 17 and 18 of Revelation comprise a unit - the chapter divisions didn't exist in the original. Chapter 17 predicts the coming destruction of Babylon; chapter 18 describes that destruction. I've also told you that chapter 18 has five basic divisions: (1) An angel announces the fall of Babylon, and gives the reasons why God's fixing to destroy her, vs. 1-3; (2) The angel warns God's people to come out of her, and also to assist in her destruction - and that's the part we've now arrived at, vs. 4-8; (3) There is great mourning and lamentation, by those who've been enjoying her sinful pleasures, and who've been enriched by her profits, vs. 9-19, which is the longest section of the chapter, and is marked by the phrase, "Alas, Babylon," which is repeated three times in the course of these 11 verses; (4) God's people are invited to rejoice over her fall, vs. 20; and (5) He final destruction is described, vs. 21-24.

The section we're now in, verses 4-8, mark the point at which God's long-suffering gives place to His justice. Last week, in examining verses 4-5, we saw four truths stated: (1) that God has some people, even in sinful Babylon - and I talked about the importance of preaching at the street dance; (2) that God wants his people to come out of Babylon, and to practice Christian separation; (3) that those who remain in Babylon will participate in her judgment; and (4) that at some point, God's patience has an end.

You'll recall that we said verse 5 pictures Babylon's sins as having been stacked so high that, like the tower of Babel, they reach unto heaven; and they make such a large pile that they're visible to God in heaven, and have attracted His attention; and so now He's fixing to do something about it. And I think I compared that to how the public schools used to operate, back when they actually tried to make the kids sit down and shut up so they could teach them something.

You'd put up with their not paying attention, and goofing off, for only so long; and at that point, you took somebody out in the hall, paddled them, and the rest of the class settled down - at least, for awhile. Today, of course, the public schools have become simply a babysitting service, and the teachers are like cops without any guns - the kids can tear the place apart and cuss the teachers out, and dare them to do anything about it.

We also looked at those words in vs. 5, "God hath remembered her iniquities." We talked about people thinking God's not going to call them to account. I think I mentioned Barak Obama, and said he seems to be getting away with a whole lot of stuff - but one day he'll be called to account. It may be on the 6th of next November, when we go to the polls - if he hasn't suspended the Constitution by that time, assuming he actually allows us to hold an election; or it may not be until judgment day, but whether the American voters call him to account or not, he'll one day give account to God - as will we all.

Anyhow, that was last week. Now, this week, we come to verses 6-7: " Reward her even as she rewarded you, and double unto her double according to her works: in the cup which she hath filled fill to her double. How much she hath glorified herself, and lived deliciously, so much torment and sorrow give her: for she saith in her heart, I sit a queen, and am no widow, and shall see no sorrow."

Before we plunge into it, I've mentioned before that, an underlying question concerning these two chapters is, who or what is meant by "Babylon"? What does "Babylon" symbolize? I've told you that, while the Catholic church maintains it stands for pagan Rome, and the Protestant reformers thought it stood for papal Rome, the Roman Catholic church, the pope and his followers, we maintain that it stands for the world system generally.

I discovered this quote the other day - it's from St. Augustine, writing in 440 A.D., or thereabouts, in his great work, *De Civitates Dei,* which means ""The City of God." Whether you ever heard of it or not, whether today's high school kids ever heard of it or not, whether the students at Southern Seminary ever heard of it or not, it was and remains one of the most influential works in the history of the Christian church, and has influenced how we all look at Scripture. Anyway, he says of this text: "Babylon is a former Rome, and Rome a latter Babylon. Rome is a daughter of Babylon, and by her, as by her mother, God has been pleased to subdue the world."

Those words were written, of course, at the time of the fall of Rome - things didn't move then quite as fast as they do now, and the destruction of Rome was an event that took several years to complete. And Augustine wrote his book while that was occurring. But he saw that the "Babylon" described in Revelation was a picture of the world system which, in his day, was the then waning Roman Empire.

Not to plunge too deeply into ancient history, but Rome was, at that time, a Christian power, and had been for a bit over a century. Despite that fact, Augustine still thought it was "Babylon," that John had been describing. Today, America is supposed to be a Christian nation - the Supreme Court is doing all it can to make us a pagan nation - but the vast majority of Americans - about 80%, in most surveys - it's a little hard to come up with the exact figure - but about 80% of Americans call themselves Christians. Like the Rome of Augustine's day, ours appears to be a Christian nation.

Augustine's point seems to have been - and because there was no First Amendment guarantee of free speech in Rome, he wasn't free to say exactly what he thought, and had to lay some of it between the lines - but his point appears to have been, that a nation could be nominally Christian, and still be the "Babylon" of Revelation 18; because, despite the pretense of religion, most of the people behaved like pagans - which is what he saw going on in his day, and what we see going on in our day.

Saturday night, a million people crowded into Times Square in New York City to see the ball drop at midnight. For entertainment, the City of New York got Lady Gaga, who entertained the crowd by singing *"Heavy Metal Lover"*; *"Marry the Night"*; and *"Born This Way."* One press account stated: "Lady Gaga took New York City's Times Square by storm Saturday for New Year's Eve, performing a medley of her hits in another shocking getup."

Need I say more? We, like Augustine, live in a society of pagans, despite the fact that America may appear to be a Christian nation. So we might well ask whether America is going to meet the same fate as the Roman Empire; or whether we, like Augustine, may actually be watching it crash down around us.

OK, so much for the excursion into ancient history. One truth which these two verses teach is, that God's punishment is proportional. As I've said before, most churches no longer do much preaching about hell - and therefore most people, even most Christians, don't have a very clear notion about what the Bible teaches on the subject.

One thing which the Bible says, and which many folks don't seem to recognize, is that the Bible says there will be degrees of punishment in hell. Not all are going to be punished alike. St. Paul wrote to the Hebrews: "For if the word spoken by angels was steadfast, and every transgression and disobedience received a just recompense of reward, how shall we escape if we neglect so great salvation?" Heb. 2:2-3. Note the words, "every transgression and disobedience received a just recompense of reward." In other words, the more one sins, the greater will be his punishment.

Jesus was standing before Pilate, the Roman governor; the crowd was just outside chanting "Crucify Him! Crucify Him." When Jesus stands mute and won't respond to Pilate's questions, Pilate asks Him: "Speakest thou not unto me? Knowest thou not that I have power to crucify thee, and have power to release thee?"

Jesus replies: "Thou couldest have no power at all against me, except it were given thee from above: therefore he that delivered me unto thee hath the greater sin." John 19:10-11. Jesus said to Pilate, "he that delivered me unto thee hath the greater sin." Note the clear meaning, "the greater sin" - difference in punishment.

In Matthew 11: 24, Jesus told the folks at Capernaum: "But I say unto you, That it shall be more tolerable for the land of Sodom in the day of judgment, than for thee." Again, note the words, "more tolerable," meaning that there's going to be a difference in punishment.

The degree of one's punishment in hell will be determined, first of all, by the number of sins he has committed. If "every transgression and disobedience received a just recompense of reward," then that means a difference in punishment, since no two people ever committed exactly the same number of sins. If one knew he were going to hell, Satan and corrupt human nature would say, "Sin and enjoy while you live." But reason and conscience would say, "Stop! Add no more to the degree of punishment in hell."

It will also be determined by one's light and opportunity. The people of Capernaum had not sinned so terribly as those in Sodom; but they had had more light, more opportunity to repent and get saved; hence, the difference in punishment, "more tolerable." And don't let you mislead you into thinking that hell won't be such a terrible place, after all; rather, it should be enough to make the blood run cold through your veins; for those who will suffer the most will be those who have had the most light, the most opportunity, to get saved, and yet have rejected the gospel and remained unsaved.

And this principle of proportionality of punishment, is clearly stated in the text before us. Verse 7 says: "How much she hath glorified herself, and lived deliciously, so much torment and sorrow give her." Let her punishment correspond with her sins. God will proportion the punishment of sinners to the measure of their wickedness.

The picture is one of a prostitute pampering her body, because she wants to sell it to customers, and what he says is, by every act of transgression and sinful pampering of the body she has been preparing for herself a suitable and proportionate punishment. Give her as much torture and grief as the glory and luxury she gave herself.

That's hard preaching - I didn't say it, St. John did - and it's the kind of preaching you won't hear at the liberal churches - but it's what the Bible says, over and over, throughout the parallel Testaments.

There's another thing I want you to see, about Babylon - her self-confidence. You've surely known people who were that way - they thought they knew it all - you couldn't tell them anything; if they were doing something the wrong say, you couldn't show them how to do it the right way - "I know what I'm doing; I don't need your help; leave me alone."

That's the picture John is painting of Babylon; and if you rush past it too fast, you'll miss it. She says, verse 7: "I sit as a queen, and am no widow, and shall see no sorrow." You wouldn't necessarily get it in the English translation - and the new translations don't catch this fine point, either. Most of them translate it exactly like the KJV, *i.e.,* "I sit a queen." The RSV does change it to say: "A queen I sit." And yet, when I was a kid, all the boys from seminary were urging folks to throw out their KJVs and get the RSV, because "it's so much clearer." Really, is "A queen I sit" easier to understand than "I sit a queen?"

But the fine point of grammar that I want to mention in passing is, that he shows her overconfidence, past, present, and future. As Bengel paraphrases it, her attitude is: "I am seated (this long time) . . . I am no widow . . . I shall see no sorrow." These words, he says, "mark her complete unconcerned security as to the past, present, and future." I suppose it's like the man who jumps off a 20 story building, and says, at each of the first 19 floors he passes, "No trouble so far."

The term "widow" may suggest a city that has been deserted - there's no one left there. The idea would be that, just as a widow was bereft of her husband, so the city would be completely bereft of inhabitants - nobody at all there. He may be suggesting "I shall never have to mourn as one bereft of her husband." And I guess it's necessary to remember that, in that day, a widow was completely without means. There was no social security, or old age pension, or food stamps - that's the way that John and his readers would have understood the term.

There's a parallel passage in Isaiah, to which John may be referring. It's in Isaiah 47, verses 5-12. I'll not read it all, but verses

7-8 say: "And thou saidst" - Isaiah is speaking to Babylon, and is predicting the fall of Babylon, even before the rise of Babylon - either that, or you have to believe, like the liberals, that Isaiah didn't really write it; that somebody else wrote it hundreds of years later, and forged Isaiah's name to it.

"And thou saidst, I shall be a lady forever: so that thou didst not lay these things to thy heart, neither didst remember the latter end of it. Therefore hear now this, thou that art given to pleasures, that dwellest carelessly, that sayest in thine heart, I am, and none else beside me: I shall not sit as a widow, neither shall I know the loss of children."

At any rate, he's picturing Babylon as self confident, not worried about anything, least of all God, or approaching judgment. Dr. Barnes says: "This is indicative of a state where there was nothing feared, notwithstanding all the indications which existed of approaching calamity."

And I do believe that's indicative of society today, not only in America, but in the world generally. The attitude is, nothing could possibly go wrong, when it's evident that there is something badly wrong. We've just passed New Years Day. I mentioned this Sunday morning, but many of you weren't there to hear it, so I'll say it again. The world is facing an economic crisis of unparalleled proportions. The only country in Europe that's got any money is Germany, and Germany's having to keep all the rest of them afloat.

Saturday night, New Year's Eve, German Chancellor Angela Merkle made a New Years speech to the German people. Sunday morning's papers carried a story that said: "German Chancellor Angela Merkle said she expects turbulence in 2012 as she does 'everything' to save the euro and end Europe's sovereign debt crisis." And it quoted her as saying: "The path to overcoming this won't be without setbacks" and that 2012 "will no doubt be more difficult than 2011."

Nor is the economy the only place where there's trouble. Sunday's Courier Journal had a story that said this: "By the time it's over, 2011 may well go down as the Year of the Test Scandal. From Waterbury to Atlanta to Asbury Park, N.J., public schools came under fire this year from media and public officials after investigations found evidence of test tampering by educators. The revelations came as schools, nearly a decade into the No Child Left

Behind (NCLB) era of test based accountability, struggled to increase the percentage of students deemed 'proficient' on state math and reading tests."

And, of course, 2011 was the year we withdrew from Iraq, after 8 years of trying to establish a stable government; and within 48 hours of the time we'd left, the president of the country was trying to have the vice-president arrested, the vice-president was on the run - and still is - and folks are asking a very reasonable question. "Is this why we sacrificed 4000 American lives and a trillion dollars? What'd we got for our money? What did those 4000 soldiers die for?"

But the thing I personally fear most of all is not the situation in Iraq, or the economic problems, or even the fact that the schools can't teach the kids anything - as serious as those problems are. Most of all, I fear the decline of religion - Bible believing churches are becoming few and far between, compared to 25 or 30 years ago, and they're all like us - they've got 20 people in a building that seats 100.

I fear the decline of morals - the rise of sodomy, the break-up of homes, the fact that most kids are being raised without any meaningful attempt at discipline; and, above all, the fact that nobody cares. Everything I've just mentioned would have caused a furor 50 years ago, or in any sane society. I've told you before, at Christmas, 1975, 36 years ago, Dr. Tom Wallace preached to our kids in chapel at Beth Haven Christian School, where I was teaching, and one thing he said was, "We live in a world gone mad." 36 years later, the situation's only gotten worse, in many ways.

Of course, the book of Revelation is a letter, which was being sent out to the seven churches in Asia Minor. One of the churches that would be reading John's letter was the church at Laodicea, to which John had written - Jesus had said, Rev. 3:17 - "Because thou sayest, I am rich, and increased in goods, and have need of nothing." One commentator renders it: "I am rich, I have acquired wealth and do not need a thing."

And whether we've been making that connection between Rev. 3 and Rev. 18, the Laodiceans certainly would have. They'd have gotten to this part, about Babylon, and seen it as another reference to themselves. We are, as Bro. Paul often reminds us, living in the Laodicean church age, when folks are lukewarm - and the church today, like the church at Laodicea, and like the folks at Babylon, has become smug, complacent, self-satisfied.

Both the folks at Laodicea, and the woman described as Babylon, were in love with the world, and the things in the world. Churches are preaching the prosperity gospel, when they ought to be preaching self-sacrifice. The harlot Babylon, certainly, was one who loved this present world, and had no thought for the next. A lot of folks, perhaps even many so-called Christians, are in that camp today.

John, who wrote Revelation, saw the matter differently. He had earlier written, in his first epistle, I John 2: 15 - "Love not the world, neither the things that are in the world. If any man love the world, the love of the father is not in him. For all that is in the world, the lust of the flesh, and the lust of the eyes, and the pride of life, is not of the Father, but of the world. And the world passeth away, and the lust thereof: but he that doeth the will of God abidteh forever."

I've already mentioned Lady Gaga's performance before a million people in New York on New Year's Eve. If you'd lived 190 years ago, in the 1820s, you'd have heard a different sort of popular music. One of the most popular pieces of the day was this - it was a popular song, but I won't attempt to sing it. The words are:

This world is all a fleeting show,
For man's illusion given;
The smiles of joy, the tears of woe,
Deceitful shine, deceitful flow __
There's nothing true but Heaven!

And false the light on glory's plume,
As fading hues of even;
And Love and Hope, and Beauty's bloom
Are blossoms gather'd for the tomb __
There's nothing bright but Heaven!

Poor wand'rers of a stormy day!
From wave to wave we're driven,
And fancy's flash and reason's ray
Serve but to light the troubled way __
There's nothing calm but Heaven!

That's what John was trying to get the Laodicean church to see, it's what America needs to realize as we enter this new year of 2012.

Rev. 18: 1-8

We return tonight to the 18th chapter of Revelation. As I've noted before, chapters 17 and 18 are a unit, describing the fate of Babylon. Chapter 17 foretells the fall of Babylon, and chapter 18 describes her fall. Chapter 18 may be divided into 5 sections: (1) an angel announces the fall of Babylon, vs. 1-3; (2) an angel warns God's people to come out of her, and to assist in her destruction, vs. 4-8; (3) there is great lamentation over her by those who have participated in her sinful pleasures, and who have shared in her profits, vs. 9-19, which is the longest section of the chapter, and is marked by the phrase, "Alas, Babylon!" which occurs three times in the eleven verses, vs. 9-19; (4) God's people are called upon to rejoice over her fall, vs. 20; and (5) the final destruction of the city is described, vs. 21-24.

And, as we've seen, "Babylon" represents the entire ungodly, humanistic, world system. We've already completed the first section, vs. 1-3, which announces the fall of Babylon; and we're in the second section, vs. 4-8, in which "another voice" - we're not told whether it's God himself speaking from heaven, or whether it's another angel - but the voice says, "Come out of her, my people." We've talked about Christian separation; I've said, and will repeat, that this is a theme which is almost totally ignored in most preaching today.

We had gotten to verses 6 - 7: "" Reward her even as she rewarded you, and double unto her double according to her works: in the cup which she hath filled fill to her double. How much she hath glorified herself, and lived deliciously, so much torment and sorrow give her: for she saith in her heart, I sit a queen, and am no widow, and shall see no sorrow."

Last week, we noted the words: "Reward her even as she rewarded you," and we said that teaches proportional punishment, a doctrine which is also taught throughout the rest of the Bible. All are not going to be punished alike in hell. The degree of their punishment will be determined, first, by the number of sins they've committed; and, second, by the amount of light and opportunity which they had.

It pictures the harlot Babylon as having "lived deliciously," which means "luxuriously, and I said that's a comparison to a prostitute, who pampers her body, because she intends to sell it to customers. It says that she's "glorified herself," which means she'd been proud and haughty. The Westminster Confession of faith begins with the words: "The chief end of man is to glorify God, and then enjoy Him forever." Most folks today don't make it their chief goal in life, to glorify God; and Babylon didn't seek to glorify God; it says that she "glorified herself," and that's what the ungodly world system, and the overwhelming majority of people in it, are doing today.

Our quarrel with the public schools is, that we have an entirely different viewpoint. Secular humanism is, by definition, humanistic, it glorifies man. The ancient Greek philosopher, Protagoras, who lived about 500 years before Christ, taught that "Man is the measure of all things." And that's what public school kids would believe, if they were actually learning anything - which I doubt.

St. Paul came to Athens, preached on Mars Hill, and told them, "You've got it all wrong. God is the measure of all things, and he's revealed to us through His Son, Jesus Christ." And when Paul told them that, it says that "some mocked," Acts 17:32 - and the public education system is still mocking, because they're a part of the world system, Babylon, that glorifies man.

Anyhow, that's some of what we talked about last week. Now, today, I want to finish verses 6-7, and go on to verse 8, and see if we can't finish this second section of the chapter, which consists of verses 4-8.

Let me return, for a moment, to this phrase that we were looking at when we closed last week, verse 7 "I sit a queen." You'll recall that I pointed out, the RSV "clarifies" the meaning, by changing it from "I sit a queen," which is what the KJV says, they make it read, "a queen I sit." And I asked whether it was really worth buying a new Bible, just to get the noun placed before the verb, instead of having the verb placed before the noun.

But, leaving that bit of liberal nonsense aside, this use of the word "sit," - the Greek word is *kathemai* - means "I govern"; I am established as the ruler." Think of the term in Col. 3:1, where Paul says: "If ye then be risen with Christ, seek those things which are above, where Christ sitteth on the right hand of God." It means, He's governing, carrying out the functions of His office. We refer to Corydon - or Bardstown, where I live - as the "county seat" meaning, it's where the government offices are located, where the county officials have their offices.

In Ezekiel 28:2, he pictures the King of Tyre as making a similar boast: "Son of man, say unto the prince of Tyrus, Thus saith the Lord God; Because thine heart is lifted up, and thou hast said, I sit in the seat of God, in the midst of the seas." So Babylon, and Tyre, and Rome, are all pictured in Scripture as having placed themselves on the throne, that rightfully belongs to God. And that's what the secular humanists who run the public education system are doing today - they've put man on the throne - and God says here, "I'm not going to allow you to do it. You're riding for a fall."

Petronius, a Roman writer who was alive and writing about this time, had a saying, *"Populus vult decipi, ergo decipiatur!"*, which means, "The people want to be deceived; therefore let them be deceived." And that is, in effect, what John pictures God as saying to the world system - you want to be deceived; OK, I'm going to send you a strong delusion, so that you'll believe a lie.

Paul writes, Romans 1:28 - "And even as they did not like to retain God in their knowledge, God gave them over to a reprobate mind." The people want to be deceived, let them be deceived. Maybe that ought to be Barak Obama's campaign slogan: "The people want to be deceived, let them be deceived."

And I suppose I would be derelict in my duty if I did not at least mention the fact that this passage is supposed by many Bible teachers to be a reference to the Roman Catholic Church's devotion to the Virgin Mary, whom it calls the "Queen of Heaven." I don't believe I've ever mentioned the subject in the five and a half years I've been teaching the Bible here; but I'm well aware of it. St. Dominic Catholic Church, in Springfield, where I grew up, has a life size statue of the Virgin Mary standing in front of the church. My oldest daughter was born in Mary Immaculate Hospital. Bro. Clellon Hays, for whom I played the piano in 1987-88, was the postmaster in

Revelation, Jeremiah says that God's going to deal with "all the kingdoms of the world, which are upon the face of the earth." And then he says, "Last of all, God's going to deal with Babylon."

So in the verse before us, John is telling us about that final wind-up of history, and gives us details of exactly how God's going to deal with Babylon, last of all. But I want you to get what Jeremiah 25 says, if you haven't read it recently; God's going to make all the nations of the earth drink of the wine of His wrath; and Babylon's going to drink last of all. And that's the point at which we have now arrived, in our journey through Revelation.

Now, in closing, let's address the question which we've been avoiding, namely, how does this square with Jesus's teaching in the Sermon on the Mount, that you should love your enemies? It seems, at first glance, to be totally inconsistent; and that's one reason most preachers avoid this chapter, and avoid most of the book of Revelation.

The answer that dispensationalists give is, that we're now in the age of grace, and this belongs to a different dispensation. Let me read you a couple of sentences that Ethelbert Bullinger wrote, which expresses that point of view:

"Is this call for vengeance given to the church? Certainly not! Nor does it belong to any period of history since the Lord's death; for the present is the day of grace. . . . This proves that Revelation 18 belongs to a future dispensation of judgment which has not yet come."

Thus Ethelbert Bullinger; and I think most premillenialists, and for that matter, most Southern Baptists, would say that, if pushed for an answer. There's probably a better explanation than that, however. The 149th Psalm - the next to last chapter in the book - says of the saints that, with "the praises of God in their mouths, and a two-edged sword in their hand," they will "execute vengeance upon the nations, even punishments upon the people, to bind their kings with chains, and their nobles with fetters of iron, to execute upon them the judgment that is written."

And then he adds, "This honor have all the saints." Psalm 149:5-9.

And, lest anyone should say, "Preacher, that's in the Old Testament," I add that Paul told the Corinthians, "Do ye not know that the saints shall judge the world?" I. Cor. 6:2 So my answer is that, when we get to chapter 19, and see the actual battle take place, it says that Jesus comes from heaven upon a white horse, v. 11; and then he adds, vs. 14 - "And the armies which were in heaven followed him upon white horses, clothed in fine linen, white and clean."

When the Beast and the False Prophet, and their allied kings and armies perish at Armageddon, the armies of the saints in heaven will take part in the terrible vengeance then to be executed. And I think that's what it's referring to. But I also believe, as I said last week, that it's a clear teaching that Christians, even in this dispensation, don't have to lie down and let the devil's crowd run over them, and that we are supposed to take what measures we can to prevent their destroying us.

In closing, let me read you something Jacob Seiss wrote, commenting on this passage, 150 years ago. "In the days of mercy and forbearance, God is not strict to mark iniquity, or to punish it at once according to its deserts. There is much that He winks at and suffers to pass for the present. But it is all written in His book, and when the final recompense comes there is no more sparing. As the sinner has measured, so it will be measured to him again. It is an awful thought, but true, that by the ills and wrongs which people do on earth they are themselves setting the gauge or measure by which they are to have judgment dealt to them at the last."

Well, I think I'm going to stop there. We've gotten through verse 6 - next week we'll begin with verse 7, and continue our study of this most critical chapter. So I hope you'll all come back then, and bring somebody else with you.

Rev. 18:1-8

Tonight we return to the 18th chapter of Revelation. You'll recall that we've seen in past weeks that chapters 17 and 18 of Revelation are a unit, and they concern the fall of Babylon. In chapter 17, Babylon's fall is foretold, and in chapter 18, her fall is described. Chapter is may be divided into five topics: (1) An angel announces the fall of Babylon, and gives the reasons why God's fixing to destroy her, vs. 1-3; (2) The angel warns God's people to come out of her, and also to assist in her destruction - and that's the part we've now arrived at, vs. 4-8; (3) There is great mourning and lamentation, by those who've been enjoying her sinful pleasures, and who've been enriched by her profits, vs. 9-19, which is the longest section of the chapter, and is marked by the phrase, "Alas, Babylon," which is repeated three times in the course of these 11 verses; (4) God's people are invited to rejoice over her fall, vs. 20; and (5) He final destruction is described, vs. 21-24.

The section we're now in, verses 4-8, mark the point at which God's long-suffering gives place to His justice. Last week, we considered verses 6-7. One point we saw last week was, that God's punishment is proportional. is clearly stated in the text before us. Verse 7 says: "How much she hath glorified herself, and lived deliciously, so much torment and sorrow give her." Let her punishment correspond with her sins. God will proportion the punishment of sinners to the measure of their wickedness.

We also saw that verse 7 pictures Babylon as saying, "I sit as a queen, and am no widow, and shall see no sorrow." I pointed out to you that, in the original, there are three verb tenses - past, present, and future. I've not had any trouble in the past; I'm doing OK now; and I'm not expecting any trouble in the future. He's picturing Babylon as self confident, not worried about anything, least of all God, or approaching judgment. I offered the opinion that America is in exactly that shape today; and I mentioned some of the things that are going on today, that ought to make us concerned. Specifically, I talked about the decline of morals in this country.

I also compared the language we read here in chapter 18 to what John said to the church in Laodicea, in chapter 3 - the language is very similar, nearly identical - and said we today are living in the Laodicean church age. And I read you a poem, written about 190 years ago, entitled, "There's nothing true but heaven." That was so in 1820, and it's true in 2012.

Anyhow, that was last week. Now, today, I want to make a few more comments about these 2 verses, verses 6-7. For one thing, it says that Babylon, which we understand to represent this entire ungodly world system, is going to bet punished, not just double, but twice that.

In the Old Testament, Exodus 22, God told Moses that, if someone were convicted of theft, he was to, not just make restitution, but to restore it double. It you'd stolen five dollars, you had to give ten back. And this principle of double restitution is found throughout the Old Testament, In Isaiah 40, for example, we read: "Comfort ye, comfort ye my people, saith your God. Speak ye comfortably to Jerusalem, and cry unto her, that her warfare is accomplished, that her iniquity is pardoned; for she hath received at the Lord's hand double for all her sins."

Isaiah's talking about the Babylonian captivity - he wrote it before Babylon even became an important power, and long before the Babylonian captivity - so prophecy it history written in advance, which proves the inspiration of the Scripture. But what Isaiah's saying is that, Israel sinned, and the Lord repaid her double - she suffered twice as much as what she'd done.

Now, I grant you, this may well be figurative language - and you know I tend to take everything literally, if you can take it literally. But in this particular case, it may be figurative language, because the sins it talks about here - *i.e.,* she's glorified herself, and lived in luxury, and been over-confident - those aren't sins that are readily quantifiable. It's not like saying, "He stole five dollars; make him give ten dollars back." These are somewhat amorphous concepts, which aren't readily quantifiable - so it may simply stand for the principle that she's to be punished completely, and to be utterly devastated.

Let me throw in something I came across this week. One of the Roman writers, who was living and writing about the same time as the New Testament was written, had a phrase: "The people want to be deceived; let them be deceived." In Latin, it sounds like a clever play on words - but that's the meaning in English. Now that is, in one sense, what god is saying here: if the people want to be deceived, OK, I'll let them. The Old Testament has a phrase, that the wicked "shall be filled with their own devices." They want to be wicked - OK, I'll let them, I'll no longer send the Holy Ghost to restrain them - and let them see how it works out. That's what's happening during the Great Tribulation, after God's Spirit is withdrawn - and things fall to pieces very rapidly.

And I think that's what's happening in America today. The people have chosen to be deceived; so God says, "OK, I'm going to let them." Someone - I think it was Edmund Burke - said that "People get the kind of government that they deserve." And I sometimes think that's what's happening in the present election cycle. People are getting the kind of government they deserve; and the Republican party may be fixing to get the kind of candidate it deserves.

I came across another quote this week. It's from a Jewish scholar named Kimchi, who lived in Spain - at the time the Arabs were running the place, by the way - there was more religious toleration in Moslem Spain than there was in Catholic Europe; *i.e.,* the Moslems were more tolerant than the pope. So, many of the Jews had fled to Spain.

But, in his commentary on Obadiah, commenting on the very first verse of the book, Kimchi said, that Obadiah was foretelling the collapse of Rome; and that when Rome fell, then Israel would rise. Now, Kimchi never heard of premillennialism, and probably hadn't even read the book of Revelation - most Jews at that day thought it was a sin to read the New Testament - but he read the Old Testament, 800 years ago, and came to the same conclusion as what John is writing here in Revelation. That at the end of the age, Rome was going to collapse, and then God was going to restore Israel. There is a unity in Scripture - and the reason most people think it's hard to understand, is because they haven't studied it very closely.

Then, I want you to note the use of the word "cup." In chapter 17, verse 4, the whore Babylon is pictured as having a golden cup in her hand, which is said to be filled with "abominations, and filthiness and fornications." Full of her sins, in other words. Now, in chapter 18:6, we read: "the cup which she hath filled, fill to her double." In other words, Babylon had made the world to drink of her cup of iniquity, has misled the world into forsaking God and sinning against Him and breaking his commandments. OK, God's got a cup for her, and God's going to give her a stronger draught than what she gave others.

I've mentioned before, the language found here, and elsewhere in Revelation - we've encountered the phrase before - is a picture of a convicted criminal being forced to drink poison. Remember, I told you about the death of Socrates, and wondered whether any of today's high school students had ever even heard of Socrates? John's readers would have known what he was talking about, even if it's not familiar to us - since we don't execute people by making them drink poison.

Incidentally, when he says she's to be given "double the double" - that's what the phrase literally says, in Greek - but it could mean that she's to be given a cup four times as big; or it could mean that the poison in it's going to be four times as strong.

There's another thing that's interesting. Where it says: "the cup which she hath filled" - it doesn't necessarily mean, pouring a liquid from one container to another, which is what the language appears to say. The word used here, is rather, the picture of a druggist mixing a medicine. When I was a kid, I've actually seen doctors and druggists, pour medicines into a small container - I think the technical term is "pestle and mortar" - and mix them together, Now, of course, the pills all come prepackaged, and all the pharmacist does is pour pills out of one bottle into another. In John's day, they still had to mix the medicines, and that's the image he's using here; of a pharmacist mixing a deadly poison. And he suggests that's what God is doing, mixing a cup of deadly poison, and He's fixing to make the world drink it.

Along that same line, there's language in Jeremiah 25, where God gives him a cup - he calls it the cup of indignation - and tells Jeremiah to make all nations drink of it. And so Jeremiah goes on for several verses, naming the different nations which are going to be made to drink of the cup of trembling - it's also called the cup of fury. One of the nations which is specifically mentioned, by the way, is "Arabia," *i.e.,* the Arab nations that are causing so much havoc around the world today. The U.S. army may not have done a very good job of defeating them; but God says He's going to.

But after he's mentioned all the other nations which are made to drink of the cup of God's fury, you'll notice that Babylon drinks last of all. At the end of history, after God has punished all the others, last of all, He comes after Babylon. Jeremiah foresaw it, 700 years before John's time - now, in Revelation, John is given additional details of how it's going to come to pass. And we today appear to be living in the last days of the present age, and may soon see the event which Jeremiah and John foretold.

Now, there's an underlying question, which I've mentioned, but have not really answered. The question is this: God appears to be speaking to His saints. "Reward her even as she rewarded you." God didn't say that to an avenging angel - Anti-Christ hadn't been persecuting the angels. The saints of God are the ones who'd been persecuted, and for the language to make any sense, you have to concede that He's saying this to His saints - *i.e.,* Babylon's persecuted you; now you go out and get even with her.

The problem is, of course, that in the Sermon on the Mount, Jesus told the disciples - and if you notice what it says at the beginning of Matthew, chapter 5, it says he was talking to the disciples; the language seems to clearly indicate that he was not talking to the multitude. But we as His disciples are instructed: "But I say unto you, that ye resist not evil. Pray for those who persecute you," and so on. Now, here, we find just the opposite - the saints he's talking to here - we believe it's not the church, but the tribulation saints - but they're told to go out and exact revenge.

How are the two notions to be reconciled? Are we to assume, like the infidels do, that the Bible's full of contradictions, and doesn't make a whole lot of sense? Are we to do like the liberals, and simply skip over this chapter; and if somebody asks you what it means, tell them, "God didn't intend for us to understand that part?" Is that the way God expects us to expound His Word?

The dispensationalists' answer has been, that it's part of a different dispensation. We live in the age of grace. At the time John's describing, the age of grace is over, and the dispensation of judgment has begun. And I suppose most Southern Baptists, if you pressed them for an answer, would probably tell you that. And I don't disagree - you've heard Bro. Paul and me talk about the dispensations, and about Clarence Larkin's book, Dispensational Truth.

But I think there's another available answer, and it's this. In the next chapter, chapter 19, we read about the return of the Lord, in glory. And after John sees Him come, riding on a white horse - it's in verse 11-13, of chapter 19 - then, in verse 14, we read: "and the armies which were in heaven followed him upon white horses, clothed in fine linen pure and white." Now, those are the saints of God, whom he's talking about; and it says that when Anti Christ is destroyed, we're going to be part of that army which destroys them. So the language of verse 6 of our text, could well be referring to that.

If so, it would accord with what Paul wrote to the Corinthians: "Know ye not that the saints shall judge the world?" In the coming

Millennial age, we're going to be the rulers - and chapter 19, is the beginning of that age - and it says that we're going to help Jesus destroy Anti Christ and his followers.

I want to point out something else before we leave these two verses. In verse 7, Babylon is pictured as saying, "I sit a queen." This may be a reference to Jeremiah, where he accuses God's people of worshiping "the queen of heaven." He uses the phrase several times. Now, we live in a community where the Catholic church is fairly strong; and you may be aware that they call Mary "the queen of heaven." It's not Scriptural; the Bible nowhere calls her that.

But here's the connection between what Jeremiah said, and what John said, and what the Catholic church says - follow me now - Jeremiah was referring to a pagan deity called Ashteroth, whom they referred to as the queen of heaven. The worship of Ashteroth continued well into Roman times. When the Roman empire converted to Christianity, the Catholic church adopted many pagan deities and practices, and simply gave them Christian titles.

And such was the case here. The worship of Ashteroth, the "queen of heaven", became the worship of the Virgin Mary, whom they called the "queen of heaven." In the last days, the Babylon which John was describing, included the one world, ecumenical church, headed up by the false prophet - and we may presume that among the pagan practices which he adopts, is the veneration of the Virgin Mary, whom they call the Queen of Heaven.

I haven't said a great deal about the Catholic church, in these years of teaching Revelation. But in my home town, St. Dominic Catholic Church had a life size statue of the Virgin Mary in front of the church - you saw it every time you drove down Main Street. My oldest daughter was born in Mary Immaculate Hospital. Bro. Clellon Hays, for whom I played the piano for quite a while, was the postmaster at St. Marys, Kentucky. And most of the Catholics in Springfield had a statue of Mary in their yard. This text at least suggests that it's a pagan practice, which will be adopted by Anti Christ and his one world church.

Let me point out something else. In vs. 7, it says: "How much she hath glorified herself." He pictures Babylon as having "glorified herself." Now, all Christians believe that, in the words of the Westminster Confession, which is the basic document of the Presbyterian Church: "The chief end of man is to glorify God."

Augustine said, "O God, Thou hast made us for Thyself, and restless are our hearts until they rest in Thee."

The ancient Greeks, the pagan Greeks, had a different philosophy. They said "The true measure of man, is man." We're not accountable to God - we're only accountable to ourselves." But John says there's a time coming when men will be glorifying themselves, exalting man, in the place of God. You've heard me speak before of "secular humanism," meaning, the worship of man instead of acknowledging God. You've heard me say, more than once, that that's what the public schools are teaching; the philosophy - the religion, if you please - of "secular humanism."

This verse suggests that it's a sign of the times. That, as the end of the age approaches, the worship of man in place of God, will increase. And, of course, Paul said that in the last days, men will be "lovers of their own selves, rather than lovers of God." And I think we're living in such a time today, and that it's a sign that we're living in the last days.

Then, looking ahead to verse 8, he says: "Therefore shall her plagues come in one day, death, and mourning, and famine; and she shall be utterly burned with fire." Her suffering will be exacerbated, will be increased, by its suddenness. In another place, it says, "For when they shall say, Peace and safety, then sudden destruction cometh upon them."

We can all remember 911- September 11, 2001. We got up that morning - it seemed like any other morning - it was on a Monday - and then a little before 9:00 a.m., suddenly the world changed, and it has not been the same since. It's been a bit over two years ago now, the folks in Port Au Prince, Haiti, were just finishing up a day of work; the Archbishop was sitting in his office at the Cathedral; tourists were sitting on the veranda at the hotel overlooking the city.

Then at 5:03 pm, the earth began to shake - and within two minutes, thousands were dead, tens of thousands homeless, and the city has not yet recovered. Those my age can remember the Kennedy assassination; those of my Dad's generation, could remember Pearl Harbor. Each of these life changing events happened suddenly, and without any warning whatever.

The fall of Anti Christ's kingdom is going to be like that. The intensity of the judgment will be magnified by its suddenness.

Well, I think I'm going to stop there. Next week, we'll begin with verse 8, which ends this section of the chapter; and we'll proceed to verse 9, which begins the third division of the chapter, the lamentation over the destruction of the city, where they cry out, "Alas, Babylon!"

Go home, read it, study it, and then come back next Wednesday, and we'll continue our consideration of this portion of the book.

Rev. 18:1-8

Tonight we return to the 18th chapter of Revelation. You'll recall that we've seen in past weeks that chapters 17 and 18 of Revelation are a unit, and they concern the fall of Babylon. In chapter 17, Babylon's fall is foretold, and in chapter 18, her fall is described. Chapter 18 may be divided into five topics: (1) An angel announces the fall of Babylon, and gives the reasons why God's fixing to destroy her, vs. 1-3; (2) The angel warns God's people to come out of her, and also to assist in her destruction - and that's the part we've now arrived at, vs. 4-8; (3) There is great mourning and lamentation, by those who've been enjoying her sinful pleasures, and who've been enriched by her profits, vs. 9-19, which is the longest section of the chapter, and is marked by the phrase, "Alas, Babylon," which is repeated three times in the course of these 11 verses; (4) God's people are invited to rejoice over her fall, vs. 20; and (5) He final destruction is described, vs. 21-24.

The section we're now in, verses 4-8, mark the point at which God's long-suffering gives place to His justice. We've been considering verses 6-7, and tonight we come to the last verse of this section, verse 8: "Therefore shall her plagues come in one day, death, and mourning, and famine; and she shall be utterly burned with fire: for strong *is* the Lord God who judgeth her."

Last week, we considered the words of a Roman adage, *si populus vult decipi, decipiatur*, which means, if the people want to be deceived, let's help them do it. I compared that to what some of the politicians in Washington are doing. We also looked at the double use made of the word "cup" in our text. In chapter 17,

There's a similar verse in Isaiah 47:14 - I'll not take the time to read it. But then, when we get to the next chapter of Revelation, chapter 19 and verse 3 - he's still talking about the destruction of Babylon - we read: "And her smoke arose up forever and ever." I also note that, in the previous chapter, chapter 17, and verse 16, it says that the beast, that is, Antichrist, and the kings allied with him, are going to assist in the destruction of Babylon. So God is going to use Antichrist to destroy the wicked, godless world system that has turned its back on Him.

Let me also share with you a sentence from Edmund Gibbon's history of Rome, THE DECLINE AND FALL OF THE ROMAN EMPIRE. He says that the early Christians believed that the Roman Empire was the mystic Babylon John was writing about, and adds:

"A regular series was prepared [in the minds of Christians] of all moral and physical evils which can afflict a flourishing nation; intestine discord, and the invasion of the fiercest barbarians from the unknown regions of the North; pestilence and famine, comets and eclipses, earthquakes and inundations. All these were only so many preparatory and alarming signs of the great catastrophe of Rome, when the company of the Scipios and Caesears should be consumed by a flame from heaven, and the city of the seven hills, with her palaces, her temples, and her triumphal arches, should be burned in a vast lake of fire and brimstone."

Then John adds, at the end of verse 8: "For strong is the Lord God who judgeth her." The language is similar to that in Jeremiah chapter 50, verses 33-34, where Jeremiah says: "Thus saith the Lord of Hosts; The children of Israel and the children of Judah were oppressed together: and all that took them captives held them fast; they refused to let them go. Their Redeemer is strong; the Lord of hosts is his name: he shall thoroughly plead their cause, that he may give rest to the land, and disquiet the inhabitants of Babylon."

David, likewise, writes: "God hath spoken once; twice have I heard this; that power belongeth unto God.

The meaning of these words of John is, that the doom of Babylon is certain because of the power of God. God is strong enough to do what He's said he's going to, and destroy Babylon. God has ample power to bring all these calamities upon her.

There is one other point about that, which I ought to share with you. The most common name for God in the Old Testament is

Elohim. It occurs 2570 times in the Hebrew Old Testament. The other word that's used frequently is *Yahweh.* In your KJV, and in most other English translations, *Elohim* is translated as "God", and *Yahweh* is translated as "Lord," printed in all capital letters.

Yahweh means, "The covenant God", but *Elohim* means "the Mighty One," God Almighty. And John's readers, being familiar with the Old Testament Scriptures, would have understood what he was alluding to. The basic idea behind the name of God, was that He was all powerful.

Now let me say something else. The verse, taken at face value, says that at the end of the age, "Babylon" is going to be destroyed by fire. The commentators through the years have pondered how that could be. Did it mean that God was going to send fire from heaven? The verse doesn't really say that; and verse 16 of the previous chapter says that Antichrist and the ten kings allied with him, "shall burn her with fire." So the source of the fire would seem to originate on earth, not in heaven. Some commentators, who thought Rome was the city meant, noted that Rome is in a volcanic area, and suggested that Rome was going to be destroyed by a volcanic eruption.

But it was one of the puzzles of Biblical interpretation. Now, for the first time, in our own lifetimes, man actually has the ability to do it. The advent of nuclear weapons makes this event possible; and the proliferation of those weapons makes the event more probable, if not inevitable. To mention but two events that are now occurring - you've seen on the news that there's been a change of leadership in North Korea. Kim il Sung, the longtime leader, has died and been replaced by his son Kim il Jong. Kim il Jong is only in his mid twenties. No one that young has ever had his finger on the nuclear trigger. When you were 21, or 25, would you have known what to do with a nuclear weapon? My youngest daughter's 27 - I wouldn't trust her with a nuclear bomb.

Iran continues working on acquiring a nuclear weapon, and by all accounts, it's evidently very close to acquiring them. It already has a missile system capable of delivering them. The Iranian dictator last week visited Venezuela and Nicaragua; and before he goes home, he's planning to stop off in Ecuador and Cuba. Cuba is 90 miles from Florida. Suppose he and Castro cut a deal for Iran to put nuclear bombs and missiles in Cuba. That would put all of us here in

Ramsey, and all the rest of the Eastern United States, within range of their missiles.

When Khruschev tried putting missiles in Cuba, almost 50 years ago, President Kennedy made him back down. Suppose Iran tries it. Is Barak Obama going to stand up to them, and keep them from doing it?

China's in the process of replacing its leadership. The old crew, that's ruled China for years, is being replaced by a new group of younger leaders, who will now have their finger on the nuclear trigger. We have no idea whether we can trust the new guys to behave responsibly. And, with Obama scaling back the United States military, we may not have the ability to do anything about it.

Here's something that appeared in today's papers: "The United States and Israel have pushed back a joint military exercise that was scheduled for the spring amid escalating tensions with Iran over that country's nuclear program. Israeli media reported that the drill was being pushed back into the second half of 2012. According to one unnamed Israeli official, the United States asked to delay the drill so it did not heighten tensions with Iran."

I could go on; but you get the point - we live in dangerous times, and unless God intervenes, men may destroy themselves. So all signs indicate that we are, that we must be, approaching the end of the age. A Presbyterian minister in New York, in 1840, wrote these lines:

We are living, we are dwelling, in a grand and awful time,
In an age on ages telling; to be living is sublime.
Hark! the waking up of nations, Gog and Magog to the fray;
Hark! what soundeth is creation's groaning for the latter day.

Will ye play, then? will ye dally far behind the battle line?
Up! it is Jehovah's rally; God's own arm hath need of thine.
Worlds are charging, heaven beholding; thou hast but an hour to fight;
Now, the blazoned cross unfolding, on, right onward for the right!

Sworn to yield, to waver, never; consecrated, born again;
Sworn to be Christ's soldiers ever, O for Christ at least be men!
O let all the soul within you for the truth's sake go abroad!

Strike! let every nerve and sinew tell on ages, tell for God.

Friends, Arthur C. Coxe wrote those words more than 170 years ago. What would he think of the world situation today? We face problems that no other generation of men has ever faced; and, sad to say, most men, even most Christians, seem totally oblivious to the danger.

Well, I'm going to leave it at that. Next week, we'll take up the dirge, the lamentation over Babylon, which is the longest section of the chapter - it runs 11 verses; it starts in verse 9, and runs through verse 19. Three different groups are seen bewailing her fall - the kings, the merchants, and the shipmasters and sailors. So go home, read the rest of the chapter, and then come back next Wednesday night, when we'll continue our study in Revelation.

Rev. 18:1-8

Tonight we return to the 18th chapter of Revelation. You'll recall that we've seen in past weeks that chapters 17 and 18 of Revelation are a unit, and they concern the fall of Babylon. In chapter 17, Babylon's fall is foretold, and in chapter 18, her fall is described. Chapter is may be divided into five topics: (1) An angel announces the fall of Babylon, and gives the reasons why God's fixing to destroy her, vs. 1-3; (2) The angel warns God's people to come out of her, and also to assist in her destruction - and that's the part we've just finished studying, vs. 4-8; (3) There is great mourning and lamentation, by those who've been enjoying her sinful pleasures, and who've been enriched by her profits, vs. 9-19, which is the longest section of the chapter, and is marked by the phrase, "Alas, Babylon," which is repeated three times in the course of these 11 verses; and that's the section that we begin tonight; (4) God's people are invited to rejoice over her fall, vs. 20; and (5) He final destruction is described, vs. 21-24.

Last week we considered verse 8. One point I made is that our actions have consequences. You can't sin and get away with it. Babylon didn't, and folks today won't either. Verse 8 mentions four calamities that are going to befall Babylon - death, mourning, famine, and "she shall be utterly burned with fire." And it says these things all befall her "in one day" - meaning, suddenly. There won't be any time to prepare. It will come at a time when they aren't expecting it.

I compared it to the bombing of Hiroshima and Nagasaki. One minute, the citizens were sitting peacefully in their homes, having breakfast - we dropped the bomb fairly early in the morning - and the next moment, 100,000 of them were dead. No warning - the devastation was so complete that it was a couple of days before Emperor Hirohito could figure out what had become of his city. And today, of course, we have bombs that make that one look like a firecracker, by comparison.

I also compared the "death, mourning and famine," to what happened in Germany - and in the other countries of Europe - after World War I in 1918. I also compared it to the destruction of Sodom and Gomorrah. I quoted Barak Obama as having said, "Change is coming," and I agreed with him - change is coming - drastic change, and it's coming very soon - but it's not the kind of change he's talking about. It's not the kind of change Jeremiah Wright preached about for those 21 years when Obama was sitting out in front of him, and now claims that he didn't hear a word Rev. Wright said.

I also read you a couple of sentences from Gibbon's Decline and Fall of the Roman Empire - and I'll bet we're the only church in the county that read from Gibbon's book last Wednesday night. Then Sunday morning, I read you a couple of sentences from "Gone With the Wind" - and I'll bet we're the only church in town that read anything from that book last Sunday. You may or may not agree with what we preach up here, but you'll have to admit that it's a little different. We expound the Bible, and the liberals don't. We tell you the truth, and the liberal churches tell you lies; and they do it in such general terms that nobody can tell for sure what they're talking about. Their motto is, "Let's be sure we don't upset anybody." These things did not Jeremiah, or Elijah, or John the Baptist, or Jesus. He didn't get crucified because he was out trying to win friends and influence people.

Jesus said to the scribes and Pharisees, "But now ye seek to kill me, a man that hath told you the truth." He said, "The reason you're trying to kill me is because I've told you the truth. You're trying to kill me, because you know I'm right."

I also talked last week about the symbolic significance of the cup. The world was enticed to drink from the cup of pleasure, and Babylon was then forced to drink judgment from that same cup. When John wrote those words, his mind must surely have gone back more than 60 years to that night when Jesus had taken the cup, and told them, "This cup is the New Testament in my blood, which is shed for you." Here, by contrast, he sees a cup representing false religion.

Well, anyway, that's some of what we said last week; now today, we begin the third section of the chapter, the lament over Babylon, that begins in verse 9, and runs through verse 19.

These 11 verses constitute what Matthew Henry calls "a doleful lamentation made by Babylon's friends for her fall." You need to understand, first of all, that in the ancient world, mourning was a much bigger deal than it is today. In our contemporary society, we tend to give the deceased a 20 minute funeral, a quick burial, and forget them. That used not to be the case. I remember my mother saying to me on one occasion, where they'd had a rather short funeral for someone; she said, "When I was a girl, and Grandfather (my great-grandfather, of course, who was a Baptist preacher) - when Grandfather had a funeral, they didn't feel like they'd given someone the proper respect, if he didn't preach for at least an hour."

You may remember that about a month ago, Kim il Sung, the longtime leader of North Korea, passed away - and the news had pictures of crowds standing in the streets and wailing - because that's the way they do it in that part of the world.

Also, in John's day, the folks - the pagans, certainly - mourned greatly, because they didn't have any hope of immortality. Paul wrote to the Thessalonians, II Thess. 4:13 - "But I would not have you to be ignorant, brethren, concerning them which are asleep, that ye sorrow not, even as others which have no hope." That's why Christians don't have elaborate mourning rituals like folks do in other parts of the world - because "he righteous hath hope in his death." Prov. 14:32 Jesus "brought life and immortality to light," II Tim. 1:10.

So we don't mourn as excessively as the folks did back then, because we have a hope, a certainty they didn't have. We know we're going to see our friends and loved ones again. Dr. Paul Horner, to whom Bro. Paul and I both had Bible classes, is the one from whom I got this poem - it was written by an English poet named John Gibson Lockhart, about 175 years ago:

It is an old belief That on some solemn shore,
Beyond the reach of grief, Dear friends shall meet once more;
Beyond the sphere of time, And sin and fate's control,
Serene in changeless prime, of body and of soul,
This creed I fain would keep, This hope I'll not forego:
Eternal be the sleep, If not to waken so.

And that is our hope, and the reason that we "sorrow not, even as others that have ho hope." But you need to read the passage against that background - in that day, mourning was a much bigger deal than it is to us in America today.

I mentioned last week that the dirge here resembles some that appear in the Old Testament prophets. One I mentioned is found in Ezekiel 26 and 27, where the prophet takes up a lament for Tyre. Let me read you one verse - it's in chapter 26 and verse 16, of the prophecy of Ezekiel. "Then all the princes of the sea shall come down from their thrones, and lay away their robes, and put off their broidered garments: they shall clothe themselves with trembling; they shall sit upon the ground, and shall tremble at every moment, and be astonished at thee."

Then come on over to chapter 32 of Ezekiel, and verses 9-10 - this time, Ezekiel has taken up a lament for Tyre - "I will also vex the hearts of many people, when I shall bring thy destruction among the nations, into the countries which thou hast not known. Yea, I will make many people amazed at thee, and their kings shall be horribly afraid for thee, when I shall brandish my sword before them; and they shall tremble at every moment, every man for his own life, in the day of thy fall."

That is somewhat the same thing that's going on here. As we consider this section of the chapter, there are several questions we should ask. One is, who are the mourners. Not long ago, I went to the funeral of one of the members of the church I used to pastor. When I got home, the first thing June asked me was, "OK, who all was there?" Well, the congregation included most of the people who'd been members of the church, back when we were there.

Who are the mourners, at the lamentation described in our text? St. John mentions three groups - and let me suggest that the number itself is significant. We've seen throughout this study that Revelation has a numbers scheme. Three is one of the numbers that recurs again and again. We've seen it before, with reference to the city of Babylon. Chapter 16, verse 19, there's a great earthquake, "and the great city was divided into three parts."

Now, here's another verse where it speaks of three things, with reference to the city. The mourners are seen to be (1) "the kings of the earth" - vs. 9; (2) "the merchants of the earth" - vs. 11; and (3) the shipmasters - vs. 17. The kings mourn their loss of power and luxury; the merchants and seamen mourn their loss of wealth through trading in the things of the world. Of course the merchants carry out their trade over the land, while the seamen carry out their trade by the sea, thus covering the whole world.

But they're all mourning the loss of things; and this contrasts with what Jesus told his disciples, Luke 12:15 - "Take heed and beware of covetousness: for a man's life consisteth not in the abundance of the things which he possesseth." The groups are first referred to in verse 3, where it talks about "the kings of the earth" and "the merchants of the earth." Then, beginning in verse 9, it sets out the details about each of them - in somewhat the same manner as a preacher may announce his three - or four, or however many - announce his points, and then go back and discuss each one of them.

The first group that it names are "the kings of the earth," verse 9. At first, you might assume that this means all the kings on earth; but look again. It mentions the ten kings, who are allied with the beast; and "the kings of the earth," who are allied with Babylon. And I'd never seen that before. I told you, when we studied chapter 17 and verse 16, that Babylon, symbolizing the entire world system, cultural and economic and religious, is first allied with the beast, symbolizing Antichrist; because in 17:3, the woman Babylon, is seen sitting upon the beast.

But then later in the same chapter, verse 16, it says that the ten kings, who are allied with Antichrist, "shall hate the whore, and shall make her desolate and naked, and shall eat her flesh, and burn her with fire." I told you that means Antichrist, after having used the world system to rise to power, will turn against that system, and seize complete and total power for himself - or will, at least, try to do so.

So there appear to be two groups of kings mentioned - those allied with the beast, Antichrist; and those allied with Babylon. In Act III scene 1 of Shakespeare's play *Julius Caesar* - the next high school kid you see, ask him - or her- whether they ever heard of William Shakespeare, or of Julius Caesar - in Act III scene 1, after Brutus and Cassius have assassinated Caesar, his friend, Marc Anthony vows to take revenge, and predicts: "A curse shall light upon the limbs of men; Domestic fury and fierce civil strife Shall cumber all the parts of Italy;" and he says that he's going to "Cry 'Havoc,' and let slip the dogs of war."

And you'd suppose that's what was about to happen here; that there was going to be a civil war of some sort between the nations allied with Antichrist, and those allied with Babylon. But it didn't happen. Babylon's allies either wouldn't or couldn't come to her defense, and now they simply stand afar off and bewail her fall. They dared not come very near. They did not even attempt to rescue her; rather, they stood by and saw her destroyed.

You've heard the term "fair weather friends"? They're your friends so long as things are going well? That's what the kings of the earth proved to be - Babylon's "fair weather friends"- when the crisis came, they cut and ran. So, they were frightened when they saw the judgments of God, and were scared to come near - but their fear was of short duration. Because in the next chapter, chapter 19 and verse 19, we see them allied with Antichrist against God, and they are destroyed, when Antichrist is destroyed.

You've probably seen people like that. They become gravely ill, they think death may be near - and they get frightened, they call the preacher, and say, "Preacher, if God will just get me out of this, I'll straighten up, I'll support the church, I'll quit drinking" - and then, when God restores them to health, their vow is forgotten, and they're back in with the devil's crowd again. That's what happens with "the kings of the earth."

Then, besides the "kings of the earth," the mourners also include the "Merchants of the earth" and the shipmasters and sailors. Many commentators refer to this aspect of the chapter as the fall of "commercial Babylon." Now, it wasn't really "commerce" - commerce is when you buy and sell things - the goods of some are exchanged for the goods of others. Babylon doesn't seem to have been exporting anything - she seemed only to be buying things. So it may not have been "commerce" in the truest sense.

But we see them stand afar off, bewailing her fall. Three times it says that they stand "afar off" - verses 10, 15, 17. Although they were afraid to come very close, yet they watched the spectacle, "fascinated by the lurid blaze," Dr. A. T. Robertson says. During John's own lifetime, the emperor Nero had set fire to the city of Rome, then stood on a hill outside town and played his fiddle while he watched the city burn. The men described here were lamenting, not fiddling, but it illustrates the fact that there's a certain fascination to standing at a safe distance away and watching a fire destroy something.

OK; so the first question, the first point is, exactly who was mourning? The answer is, three groups. Second question, How were they mourning? Your KJV says they "shall bewail her, and lament for her." The first word, *klio,* translated "bewail" means that they were giving audible expression to their grief. They weren't just crying quietly to themselves. It can mean that they were "wailing" or "howling" or "singing a dirge."

The second word, *kopto,* translated "lament," - well, this is another place where the English translation doesn't quite capture the meaning of the original - it means "to smite the breast." It's the same word that Jesus used in Matt 24:30 and Luke 23:27, and Rev. 1:7, to describe the grief that's going to take place at the Lord's second advent.

It's also interesting to note that, in verse 9 where it's talking about "the kings of the earth," it says "shall bewail and lament" - the verb it in the future tense. In verse 11, although your KJV renders it "shall weep and mourn", in the original the verb is in the present tense, indicating that they are doing it, right then, while John's watching them. Then in verse 19, it says that they "cried, weeping and wailing," past tense, as though it had already happened. Bullinger comments: "It is as though a moving scene is passing before the eyes, while the interpreting angel explains it."

Every word is inspired, every word is important, right down to the tenses of the verbs, I don't care what the folks over at Southern Seminary taught me when I was a student there. We believe in the plenary, verbal, word-for-word inspiration of the Scriptures. And then, they mourn saying "Alas, alas!" The expression is found three times - in verses 10, 16 and 19. It denotes, Thayer's Lexicon says, an "evil, the infliction of which is deplored."

The Greek word is *ouai,* so that if you were reading it in Greek, the expression would be *ouai, ouai.* It sounds like the cry a bird would make. I mention that point because, back in Rev. 8:13, we saw an eagle flying through the midst of heaven, crying "Woe, woe, woe, to the inhabiters of the earth by reason of" the three trumpets which had yet to sound. Remember we studied that, almost 4 years ago?

And then, it's interesting to compare the world's reaction to the destruction of Babylon, with its reaction to the deaths of the two witnesses, back in chapter 11, verse 10: "And they that dwell upon the earth shall rejoice over them, and make merry, and shall send gifts to one another; because these two prophets tormented them that dwelt on the earth."

When the two witnesses were killed, the world rejoiced; but when Babylon is destroyed, the earth mourns. Jamieson, Faussett and Brown comment: "Contrast the world's rejoicing over the dead bodies of the two witnesses who had tormented it by their faithfulness, with its lamentations over the harlot who had made the way to heaven smooth."

So, we've seen who is mourning, and how they're mourning; now let me call your attention to who's not mourning, namely, the saints, apostles, and prophets - those whom Babylon has been persecuting. Quite the contrary - not only are they not mourning - in verse 20, they are admonished to "rejoice over her;" which they proceed to do, in the first verses of chapter 19. Look at 19:3 - "And again they said, Alleluia. And her smoke rose up for ever and ever."

In his documentary about the Civil War, Ken Burns pictures a former slave, who has then joined the Union army, encountering his former master, who had fought for the Confederacy, and is now a prisoner of war. So the former slave is now a guard, and his former master is now his prisoner. In the movie, the slave says to his former master, "Why, hullo, Massa; looks like tha bottom rail on the top now!"

That's what's happening here in Revelation; both Babylon and Antichrist have been persecuting the church; then suddenly the tables are turned, and the church is reigning with Christ, while

Babylon is already destroyed, Antichrist and his allies are fixing to be. I don't think they had rail fences that day in time; but that's what's happening here - "De bottom rail on the top this time!"

Then, we might ask, when are they mourning? Think of someone dying, and the funeral home announcing, "Visitation will be from 7 to 9 p.m." The book of Ecclesiastes says that there's "a time to mourn." When are they mourning? Note verse 10: "For in one hour is thy judgment come!" In verse 8, it says: "Therefore shall her plagues come in one day!" Both phrases are intended to emphasize the suddenness of the calamity.

You may remember that when Daddy Bush - Bush 41 - invaded Kuwait, and threw Saddam Hussein's army out, they started amassing troops along the border, in July - and they brought in more troops and more equipment, month by month - until February, when they finally invaded. My son-in-law Ricky was one of those soldiers - and they stayed in the encampment there for months. Saddam knew it was coming - there was no particular surprise when they finally did.

Babylon's destruction is going to be just the opposite. Verse 10 says it will come "In one hour." Paul wrote to the Thessalonians, I Thess. 5:3 -"For when they shall say, Peace and safety; then sudden destruction cometh upon them, as travail upon a woman with child; and they shall not escape."

Well, I think I'll leave it there, and take it up again next week. We've seen who the mourners are, where they are, how they're mourning, who's not mourning, and when they're mourning. Next week we'll take it up there and ask why they mourned. What they were mourning for, and what they were not mourning for? So go home, read Rev. 18, verses 9-19, ask God to show us what they mean, and then come back next Wednesday night, and we'll discuss them.

Rev. 18: 9-19

Tonight we return to the 18th chapter of Revelation. As you may recall, we've seen that chapters 17 and 18 of Revelation are a unit - they're both concerned with the fall of Babylon. Chapter 17 foretells the fall of Babylon, and chapter 18 describes her fall. We are considering chapter 18 under five heads: (1) an angel announces the fall of Babylon, and gives the reasons why God's destroying her - vs. 1-3; (2) an angel warns God's people to come out of her, and calls on them to assist in her destruction - vs. 4-8; (3) there is great mourning and lamentation by those who've been enjoying her pleasures, and who've been enriched by her commerce - vs. 9-19, which is the longest section of the chapter; (4) God's people are invited to rejoice over her fall, vs. 20; and (5) her final destruction is described, vs. 21-24.

We've now covered the first two of those divisions, including verses 1-8, and last week we began our consideration of the third section, which runs from verse 9 to verse 19, which is the dirge, the lamentation over Babylon's fall. It's marked by the phrase "Alas, Babylon!" which occurs three times in the eleven verses of the dirge. Last week we asked several questions about the lament: first, who are the mourners - and the answer is, three groups are identified as mourning and bewailing Babylon's fall, namely, the Kings, the merchants, and the seamen and sailors.

Second, where are they mourning? And the answer is, they're "standing afar off" - they are so frightened by the judgment of God that they dare not come very near. Third, how are they mourning? The answer is that they're pictured as being so upset that they're beating their breasts; and we compared their wailing over Babylon's fall with their celebrating when the two witnesses were killed, in Revelation 11.

Fourth, who's not mourning - and the answer is, the saints of God - they're rejoicing over Babylon's fall. Fifth, When are they mourning? The answer is, "in one hour"; and then on down in the chapter it says, "in one day"; so the picture if of sudden destruction - no time to prepare. I think I mentioned our 7 months build-up before we attacked Saddam Hussein, in 1992 - he knew perfectly well that we were coming - there was nothing unexpected about it. And I compared that with our bombing of Hiroshima, when no one had any clue it was coming, and 100,000 people were incinerated, without ever knowing what had hit them.

I've said, repeatedly, that Babylon represents the entire corrupt world system - economic, cultural, religious. There's a battle going on between us and them; and most churches aren't honest enough to tell you that. The liberal churches tell us we've got to get along with the world, and not make anybody mad. That's not the message of Revelation 18 - or anywhere else in the Bible.

Anyhow, that's where we were last week. Now today, I want to begin by asking a couple of more questions about the lament over Babylon. One is - and I guess this is question six - we covered five different questions last week. So question six is, "What are they mourning?" The answer is clear, of course. They are mourning the fall, the ruin of Babylon, of the present world system. I make this point in order to say, that they're mourning the wrong thing. They are mourning, not her sin, but her ruin.

There are a lot of things in America today that folks ought to be concerned about. Last week - Monday, a week ago, on the 23rd of the month, tens of thousands of people came to Washington, D.C., and demonstrated in favor of the right to life - demonstrated against abortion. Did you see any coverage of that in the press? Did the Courier Journal, or NBC News, or anybody else, run a story about that demonstration? Of course not; people aren't concerned about right and wrong. They're concerned about money.

We have one Presidential candidate who's saying, "You should elect me because I've made a lot of money." And he's found voters very receptive to that message. Why? Because most people care a lot more about money than they do about principles. As the end of the age approaches, that's only going to get worse - until, at the end of the age, the kings, and the merchants, and the seamen, pictured here, care not a whit about Babylon's sins - but they're greatly concerned because their hope of gain is gone.

Have you read the 16th chapter of Acts lately? Paul and Silas are in Philippi, and they cast the demon out of an afflicted girl. She'd been "soothsaying" - she'd been a fortune teller, and her masters had been making a lot of money off her. So when Paul casts the demon out of her, and she quits serving Satan, it says, vs. 19: "And when her masters saw that the hope of their gain was gone," they had Paul and Silas thrown in jail. They didn't care that the afflicted girl had been healed. They only got upset when "the hope of their gain was gone."

The same thing's happening in the book of Revelation, chapter 18 - and the same thing's happening all around us, every day. As you know, we weren't able to have church Sunday morning, because the million. We couldn't have done that; I doubt that Lonnie Mattingly's church, or Southeast Christian, could have written a check in that amount.

The Reformation fathers were particularly angered by the Catholic Church's having sold what it called "indulgences," which was a piece of paper which was supposed to guarantee that you'd go straight to heaven when you died, without having to stop in purgatory before you got there.

On the other hand, maybe the meaning is symbolic. "Babylon" is symbolic - he wasn't talking about a real, physical, flesh and blood whore by that name. So maybe the list of Babylon's merchandise is, likewise, only symbolic. If so, what it indicates is that the world's false religious system, and the world system in general, "did not witness against carnal luxury and pleasure-seeking, the source of the merchants' gains, but conformed to them. She cared not for the sheep, but for the wool. Professing Christian merchants in her lived as if this world, not heaven, were the reality, and were unscrupulous as to the means of getting gain."

There was a movie that came out back in 1964 called "The Pleasure Seekers." That phrase captures much of what contemporary American society is all about. Most folks have no greater goal in life, than just to have a good time. When I was in teachers college, they told us, "Now, one of the main goals of education is to train kids how to spend their leisure time." Public schools are being called on to provide more and more programs, to help kids pass their leisure time.

What leisure time? The night we organized Temple Church, Dr. John Haycox preached at our tent meeting. I don't remember most of what he said, but he did say one thing that's stuck with me. He said, "You're not going to have any spare time, if you do your duty to your employer, and to your family, and to God." He said those words 45 years ago, and they're just as true today as they were the night when he spoke them. Having too much leisure time, and not knowing what to do with it, has become the curse of America.

Anyhow, then after verse 11, in verses 12-14, we have a list of things that they used to sell to Babylon, but no one is able to buy any more. It's a sort of inventory. Before the age of computers, most stores took inventory once a year. They'd close the store for a day or two, and go through the whole place, and write down a list of everything in the store. I helped them do it a number of times at the dry goods store where my folks worked. You'd get a pad or a notebook, and start at the front door and work your way back, writing down what all you had in stock. "Five pairs of men's socks. Ten pairs of ladies shoes. 50 spools of white thread."

That's what this is - it's an inventory, setting out a list of what merchandise they had left on hand when Babylon collapsed, and which they could no longer sell; there was nobody who could buy it, because the economy had collapsed, like the American economy seems to be doing. It lists 29 items, and they're arranged in some sort of order, if you can figure out exactly what categories John had in mind. One commentator divides them into seven groups: (1) treasures - which includes gold, silver, precious stones, and pearls; (2) fancy fabrics - which includes fine linen, purple , silk and scarlet cloth; (3) fancy building materials, which includes citron wood, articles made of ivory, costly wood, bronze, iron, and marble; (4) spices and related items, which includes cinnamon and spice, of incense, myrrh, and frankincense; (5) foods, which includes wine and olive oil, fine flour, and wheat; (6) livestock, which includes cattle and sheep, horses and carriages; (7) slaves, which includes the bodies and souls of men.

There are a couple of things to be noted; all appear to be imports; Babylon doesn't appear to be exporting anything. In today's terminology, we'd say they have "a balance of payments deficit;" like we have with crude oil, for example - we import a lot of it, and export none of it.

And then you'll also notice that they're all luxury goods. It's not the type of stuff that poor folks would buy; not the kind of stuff you'd be apt to find at Wal-Mart of J.C. Penny. So the picture is of a city that is wealthy, lazy, and self-indulgent. And, I say again, we might well ask whether that's how our civilization is becoming.

I think I'm going to stop there - we've gotten through verse 11; next week we'll take it up at verse 12, and look at the list of things that Babylon had been splurging on. I don't really intend to preach a 29 point sermon - since I usually don't preach more than about 20 minutes, I'd have to talk real fast, and only spend about 50 seconds on each point. But we'll at least hit the highlights of verses 12-14 next week, and then proceed from there, time permitting.

You've probably never heard a 29 point sermon before - Bro. Paul did preach an 18 point sermon up at Temple once - maybe that's why they chased us off. And you may never hear a 29 point sermon again - so if you miss next week, you may wish you'd been here. And so we'll take it up there next Wednesday.

Rev. 18:9-19

Tonight we return to the 18th chapter of Revelation. You'll recall that we've seen in past weeks that chapters 17 and 18 of Revelation are a unit, and they concern the fall of Babylon. In chapter 17, Babylon's fall is foretold, and in chapter 18, her fall is described. Chapter 18 is may be divided into five topics: (1) An angel announces the fall of Babylon, and gives the reasons why God's fixing to destroy her, vs. 1-3; (2) The angel warns God's people to come out of her, and also to assist in her destruction - and that's the part we've now arrived at, vs. 4-8; (3) There is great mourning and lamentation, by those who've been enjoying her sinful pleasures, and who've been enriched by her profits, vs. 9-19, which is the longest section of the chapter, and is marked by the phrase, "Alas, Babylon," which is repeated three times in the course of these 11 verses; (4) God's people are invited to rejoice over her fall, vs. 20; and (5) He final destruction is described, vs. 21-24.

We're now slogging our way through the third of these five sections, the lament over Babylon's fall, set out in verses 9-19. That's the section that's most familiar; and most people, if you ask them what Revelation 18 is about, will tell you it's a dirge, a lamentation that goes "Alas, Babylon!" Actually, the chapter has 24 verses, and that accounts for only 10 of them; but it's the central section of the chapter, and the other 14 verses are either leading up to, or summarizing, what's set out in those 10 verses. So, we're now at the heart of the chapter.

To this point, we've asked and answered several questions about the dirge, the lamentation: (1) who's mourning - and the answer is, three groups - the kings, the merchants, and the shipmen and sailors. (2) where are they mourning? The answer is, they're "standing afar off", either because they're unwilling to come to Babylon's aid, or maybe because they're scared to. (3) How are they mourning? Answer, they're beating their breasts in anguish - which indicates how completely devastated they are. (4) Who's not mourning? Answer, the saints of God - they're rejoicing over her fall. (5) When are they mourning? Answer, "In one hour," meaning, her devastation came suddenly and unexpectedly. (6) What are they mourning? And the answer is, they're mourning the wrong thing. Instead of mourning over her sins, they're only mourning over her fall. They're not sorry they did wrong - they're only sorry that they got caught. (7) Why are they mourning? We spent most of the time last week addressing that question; and the answer is, in brief, they're mourning because the present world system is gone, and that's all they had. They loved the world - remember, we read the verses from First John, about not loving the world, or the things in the world? They loved the world, and when it disappeared, they had nothing left.

We as Christians are not to love the world - ours is an other-worldly gospel - but many churches today are preaching a message - it's not the gospel - but are proclaiming a message that's all about this world - how to get your body healed, how to get rich, how to get your civil rights. I brought you an article Sunday about Jessie Jackson demonstrating at the Grammy Awards, because they weren't awarding enough prizes to minority groups. Now, friends, that's not an "other-worldly" gospel. Can you really see Jesus doing that? Can you really see St. Paul doing that? Can you really see John sitting on Patmos, and writing to the seven churches, about who's going to win the Grammy Awards?

Anyhow, that was last week. Now, as we closed last week, I directed your attention to the list of things set out in verses 12 and 13, that are no longer being bought and sold. There are 29 of them, in total, and I suggested the possibility of a 29 point sermon. So I hope you either have your pencil and paper ready to write down all 29 points, or else that you have a good memory, so that you can remember all 29. Actually, I only intend to hit the high points, and then go on. I suppose most preachers would be content to just skip over this list, like we do over the genealogies, and go on to something else. But since we believe every single word's inspired, my soul, Soul, thou hast much goods laid up for many years; take thine ease, eat, drink, [and] be merry." The rich fool would have fitted right in to the society of Babylon; and he would fit into the society of contemporary America."

The year I was a senior in high school, they required us to take psychology - if I hadn't been forced to, I wouldn't have, because I thought then, and think now, that the psychiatrists and psychologists are all a bunch of fakes and frauds, who ought to be in jail. But the school principal, who taught the psychology class, was telling us one day, "Now, we want all you kids to be successful. It's very important that you succeed in life."

So, being a pest, I asked him, "Prof, how can you measure success? How can we know whether we've succeeded or not?' And without any hesitation whatever, Prof responded, "You measure success in terms of money." He told me that in 1962 - the public schools were teaching that, 50 years ago - and they still are. That's not what this Book says. Are the public schools teaching Biblical values, or are they teaching the values of Babylon?

And where it uses the word "fruits" in verse 14 - the reference obviously is to the 29 things listed in verses 12-13 - but the word "fruits" - *opora* - has a precise meaning in the original - it refers specifically to "ripe summer fruit" that's ready to be picked, and if you don't go ahead and pick it, it's going to go bad. So the reference is to a world that is ripe for judgment.

And the verse says that the loss is final and irremediable. The Greek term which is translated "no more at all," - it's three words, actually, *ouketi ou me* - but the English translation "no more at all," doesn't capture the meaning of the Greek particularly well - the words mean something like "no not never" - we don't use that many negatives in a row in English - but it's the strongest expression of negation of which the Greek language is capable. And it not only implies that they won't be recovered, but it also implies the notion "don't even think about it." I'm not criticizing the King James Version - but any time you translate stuff from one language into another, there are some passages that lose a bit of their "wallop" in the translation. The New Living Bible, which I usually don't like, paraphrases this verse as saying: "The fancy things you loved so much are gone," they cry. "All your luxuries and splendor are gone forever, never to be yours again." And while that may not be a word-for-word translation, it captures the sense of the original fairly well.

It's also obvious that the merchants spoken of here had compromised and colluded with Antichrist, in order to make a lot of money. You'll recall that we read in Rev. 13: 17 that, when Antichrist came to power he made a law "And that no man might buy or sell, save he that had the mark, or the name of the beast, or the number of his name." So, when Antichrist comes along, he forbids people to worship God, and orders them to worship him, instead, and enforces the regulation by saying that you can't continue to operate your business unless you join my religion and recognize me as god.

So all the merchants of the world are faced with a choice, and some refuse to take the mark of the beast, and he forces them out of business. The ones who remain in business, the ones pictured here, wind up making a lot of money, but in order to do so, they've had to cooperate with Antichrist, and help him stamp out God's people and the true religion.

The same thing happens today. Obama issued a regulation just last week, that if the Catholic church wants to keep operating its hospitals, they have to offer contraceptive services of all kinds, including the so-called "morning after" pill, which is simply another way of inducing an abortion. So religious leaders face a choice. Dr. Mohler, President of Southern Seminary in Louisville, issued a statement a week ago today in which he said: "You at least have to admire the courage of the Roman Catholic bishops in saying they are willing to go to jail rather than to comply with this. How many evangelical presidents and pastors and leaders will be willing to do the same? We're going to find out in the coming months."

And it's happening in every area of life. Lester Roloff had been operating several children's homes in Corpus Christi, Texas, for decades. Then one day the Texas governor at the time, Democrat Anne Richards, sent the goons and cutthroats from Child Protective Services in, and told him, if you want to keep operating, you're going to have to let us tell you how to run your children's homes. We'll make the rules, and tell you what you can do and what you can't do." He said, "I'm not going to do it."

So Anne Richards and her gang put him in jail - five separate times - and eventually managed to close him down. The time comes

Well, that takes us through the first two categories; five more to go; so we'll finish them next week, and then move on. The picture he's drawing is one of opulence - of excessive wealth - and also of immorality. And so, to determine whether we're living in the last days, and whether contemporary society fits the description of Babylon, we have to ask whether it's characterized by excessive luxury, over-indulgence of the flesh, and by immorality. I don't think there's much doubt, on either score, that America, and Western society generally, fits the description quite well.

The merchants of Babylon got rich by being willing to sacrifice principles for money. Isn't that what America's doing today? Isn't that why we have a gambling boat down on the river? Isn't that why we have abortion mills, like the one where Brother Ron goes and pickets every Saturday? And so far as immorality, most of us here can remember 50 or 60 years ago - and evil wasn't nearly so wide open as it is today. Compare the movies today with the ones John R. Rice preached against back in the 1930's. Compare the filth and junk that's on TV today, with the shows that were on 50 years ago.

Compare contemporary music, or what passes for music, with the music of a generation or two ago. When Elvis first came along, the preachers said his performances were lewd and suggestive - but what's going on today makes Elvis and the other singers of that time look mild by comparison.

Well, I said I was going to stop, and I will. We'll take it up next week at verses 12-13 of chapter 18, and continue through the chapter. Be sure you come back, and bring some folks with you, and I'll see you here then.

Rev. 18:9-19

Tonight we return to the 18th chapter of Revelation. You'll recall that in the past weeks we've seen that chapters 17 and 18 of Revelation are a unit, and they describe the fall of Babylon - which, I told you, represents the ungodly world system - cultural, educational, political, economic. The chapter has five sections: (1) An angel announces the fall of Babylon, and gives the reasons for her fall -

verses 1-3; (2) The angel warns God's people to come out of her, and to assist in her destruction - verses 4-8; (3) There is great mourning and lamentation by those who have been enjoying her sinful pleasures, and who have been enriched by her profits - verses 9-19, which is the longest section of the chapter, and the section at which we have now arrived; (4) God's people are invited to rejoice over her fall, verse 20; and (5) Babylon's final destruction is described, verses 21-24.

As I say, we've now reached the third section, which is the longest - it runs eleven verses - and it's a dirge, a lament, over the fall of Babylon. Three groups are said to lament her fall - the kings, the merchants, and the ship owners and sailors. We've now talked about the lament of the kings, and when we quit last week, we were discussing the lament of the merchants. In verses 12 and 13, there is a list of 29 items - and they're all luxury goods - not the type of things poor folks like us would have had - none of those John was writing to actually owned any of the things listed. And I was trying to hit the high points of the things named in the list of things that could no longer be bought and sold, since Babylon was no more.

There are 7 categories of things listed - and dividing them into categories may make it easier for you to remember, and to deal with. First, it mentions "treasures" - four are listed - "gold, silver, precious stones, and pearls." We discussed them last week. Second, "fancy fabrics" - four are mentioned - "Fine linen, purple, silk, and scarlet cloth." And we discussed them last week.

That brings us to the third category of goods - fancy building materials, of which there are six. The first mentioned is "thyine wood." It's the only time the word translated "thyine" appears in the New Testament, and scholars don't agree whether the tree meant was some sort of a cedar, or was a citrus of some sort - but it had to be imported from across the Mediterranean - what is today the country of Libya. So "thyine wood" was quite expensive, and only the rich could afford it. The wood was colorful - Dr. A. T. Robertson says the wood resembled "a peacock's tail, or the stripes of a tiger, or panther." It's said to have been used to make statues and furniture; it also had a sweet small, and could be burned for use as incense.

The word translated "wood" can also mean "tree," and in that connection is used to describe the tree of life that's said to grow in heaven - Rev. 22:2. The word is also used in three places to describe the cross of Jesus Christ - I Peter 2:24 says: "Who his own self bare our sins in his own body on the tree," and in Acts 5:30, Peter tells the High Priest and the Sanhedrin - which was like the U.S. Supreme Court and Congress and the President, all rolled up into one - he tells them: "The God of our fathers raised up Jesus, whom ye slew and hanged on a tree."

People criticize us for being too personal, and saying things that might hurt somebody's feelings - I suppose the High Priest, and the folks who'd just a few weeks before crucified Jesus, might have taken Peter's words as criticism of what they'd done. So when we criticize the national leadership, I think we're on pretty firm Biblical ground. But my point is, again, that most of these items, that Satan was using in Babylon, are also said to have been used by God - so Satan has a clever imitation of God's works.

And then it says: "all manner vessels of ivory." The Greek word is "*elephantinos*," from which our word "elephant" comes. It's the only time this word occurs in the New Testament, although in the Old Testament, we are told that Ahab had a palace made out of ivory, I Kings 22:39. It comes, of course, from the tusk of an elephant, and was obviously hard to procure, and was valuable then, as it still is today.

Then it mentions "all manner vessels of most precious wood." It means furniture, made out of costly wood. I grew up living over a furniture store - it belonged to my uncle - Bro. Paul knows who I'm talking about. And then, last spring, when I finally got a little settlement money for my auto accident, my wife said, "I want to go shopping for furniture." So we went to a place that was supposed to have furniture at a discount - and I really wasn't prepared for how much the price of furniture had gone up, since my uncle got out of the furniture business 25 years ago.

Then, it mentions "brass, iron and marble." This is the only place in the New Testament where the word "marble" occurs. We know the Romans used marble for making statues, because some of them are still around. As for "brass," we are told, in the first chapter of Revelation, that when John saw Jesus, "his feet [were] like unto fine brass, as if they burned in a furnace." And we're told twice in the book of Revelation, that Jesus is going to rule the nations "with a rod or iron." And in chapter 2, verse 27, we're told that "he that overcometh" shall rule the nations "with a rod of iron." So, once again, Satan has put forth his imitation of what God has prepared for his people.

The fourth category of Babylon's merchandise is "spices, and similar items," and it names four: "cinnamon, and odours, and ointments, and frankincense." Cinnamon came from South China - so it had to be transported a very long distance, and was, accordingly, quite expensive. The Old Testament mentions it as having been used to make the oil with which the high priest was anointed. But in Proverbs 7:17, we find the prostitute using it to entice young men into her lair.

The word translated "spice" means a fragrant plant from India, which was used for perfume - so it also had to be brought in from a long distance away, and was very expensive. "Incense" has been mentioned twice before in the book of Revelation - in chapter 5, verse 8, and again in chapter 8 verses 3-4, it's said to be mingled with the prayers of the saints, at the altar before God's throne. You will all recall that one of the gifts which the Wise Men brought to the child Jesus was frankincense. And in Malachi 1:11, we read that, during the millennium: "From the rising of the sun even unto the going down of the same my name shall be great among the Gentiles; and in every place incense shall be offered unto my name." So, once again, we observe that Satan has his imitation, his counterpart, of the things that are used for the worship of God.

The fifth category of things found in Babylon is foods - it mentions "wine, and oil, and fine flour, and wheat." As to the flour, this is the only place in the New Testament that the word occurs, and there's a reason. Flour, of course, is made out of wheat - and it was more expensive than barley or rye. So when the boy brought his lunch to Jesus, in John chapter 6, it contained "five barley loaves."

Do you remember that, back when we were studying the 7 seals, in chapter 6 of Revelation, we read: "A measure of wheat for a penny three measures of barley for a penny." What does that tell you - that wheat was three times as expensive as barley - and that was before it had even been ground into flour - so only the rich could afford to eat bread made out of wheat. The meaning would have perfectly clear to John's readers in the seven churches, even if it's not obvious to us.

In that same verse, Rev. 6:6, it goes on to say, "and hurt not the oil and the wine." The "oil" mentioned here is not petroleum - they didn't have cars - but olive oil, which was made from olives. It was used for cooking, also for burning in lamps - think of the five foolish virgins who forgot to take any oil for their lamps; it was used for medicinal purposes - think of the good Samaritan who bound up the man's wounds, pouring in oil and wine; and it was used for anointing priests, and kings.

In Revelation 6, under the second seal, while the price of foodstuffs - wheat and barley - rise to impossibly high levels, the price of oil and wine does not - you could still get them. However, here at the end of the tribulation, they aren't available either. So, under the reign of Antichrist, things have gotten worse, not better. Does that remind you of any politicians we know about - they get elected promising to make things better, and instead things get worse?

Then, the sixth category livestock - "beasts, and sheep, and horses, and chariots." The word translated "beasts" could mean cattle, but since it's mentioned along with "chariots", it probably means "beasts of burden" which could carry a load, or pull a wagon. The word "horse" occurs fifteen times in the book of Revelation, and only one other time in the New Testament, which probably reflected the fact that poor folks, which the early Christians were, couldn't afford horses. It was something only rich people had.

The word translated "chariots" means a horse-drawn conveyance that had four wheels, and it was used for riding in, rather than for hauling stuff.

Then, finally, the seventh category is "slaves, and souls of men." The reformation fathers, who thought Babylon represented the Roman Catholic Church, believed that this meant: "Popery has derived its greatest gains from the sale of masses for the souls of men after death, and of indulgences purchased from the Papal chancery."

The religious liberals take this as a condemnation of slavery. If you were at Sunday School Sunday morning, you'll remember that I said the Bible does not condemn slavery. Those who think it should, try to read this verse as an implicit repudiation of slavery. One commentator writes: " Though the New Testament does not directly forbid slavery, which would, in the then state of the world, have incited a slave revolt, it virtually condemns it, as here."

I'm not sure I agree with either of the two. The Greek word translated "slaves" is *"soma"*, which simply means "body." John's meaning seems to be that, in Babylon's eyes, they were just bodies, to add to the long list of saleable merchandise, alongside the horses and the chariots. In Ezek. 27:13, Ezekiel says of Tyre, that "they traded the persons of men and vessels of brass in thy market." In other words, the bodies of the slaves were just another item of merchandise. But then John adds the barb, "slaves, and the souls of men." In other words, they're bodies that have souls. They're not just another article of merchandise. And that would have rung a bell with those he was writing to, because many of them either were slaves, or had been slaves. But it's a point that would have slipped past the Roman censor, since it comes at the end of a long list or items that he wasn't particularly interested in, and may not have read very carefully.

Today we don't have slavery - but we do have abortion. And we, as Christians, believe that each aborted baby is a body which has a soul. Whereas, to the abortion doctors, they're just an article of merchandise, something they can make money off of. And in November, we need to elect a President who agrees with us, and not with them.

Another way of reading those last two items, which in Greek says "the bodies and souls of men," is to assume that it's another way of saying, when Babylon disappears, she takes down with her every freedman, as well as every slave. And certainly death is a leveler - when destruction comes, it takes down the rich and powerful right along with the poor and the powerless.

Well, then after the list of 29 things, there's a little more of the dirge, the merchants lamenting for their loss; look at verses 15, through the first part of verse 17: " The merchants of these things, which were made rich by her, shall stand afar off for the fear of her torment, weeping and wailing, And saying, Alas, alas, that great city, that was clothed in fine linen, and purple, and scarlet, and decked with gold, and precious stones, and pearls! For in one hour so great riches is come to nought.

These verses say, very simply, they say three things - Babylon's fall is sudden, it's complete, and it's irreversible. It is, first of all, sudden - it's said in verse 17, to have come "in one hour"; back in verse 8, her ruin is said to have come, "in one day." Is that a contradiction in the Bible? I think not; the angel says to John that Babylon's destruction is going to come "in one day;" but, to the terrified merchants standing afar off, her ruin comes so suddenly and so unexpectedly that it appears to have happened "in one hour," real fast. They're so scared, that they exaggerate how fast it's happened.

Second, her ruin is said to have been not only sudden, but also complete. In verse 14, she's said to have lost "all things which were goodly and dainty," and here in verse 17, she's said to have "come to nought." The Greek word - and in the original, it's just one word, which in English is rendered as a phrase - the Greek word id *eremoo*, and the basic idea is that it'll become a desert - nobody there anymore - completely quiet and deserted.

Last Sunday was Abraham Lincoln's birthday. He grew up in a small town about 65 miles west of here - it's today called Lincoln City, Indiana, and is down past Jasper. Fifteen years after he'd grown up and gone off to Springfield, Illinois to practice law, he decided to go back and visit the old home place. What he found was that the town was almost completely gone - there was only one guy still living there, and he was crazy. Everybody else he'd known was buried in the cemetery - his mother was buried there.

And Lincoln wrote a poem about it - the last few lines of it go, that "every sound appears a knell, and every spot a grave. I range the fields with pensive tread, and pace the hollow rooms; And feel (companion of the dead) I'm living in the tombs." Well, Lincoln was a very melancholy man, all of his life. But that's how the merchants who'd used to do business in Babylon, felt - there was nothing left - the ruin had been sudden, and it was complete.

Isaiah and Jeremiah both compare the coming destruction of Babylon to God's having destroyed Sodom and Gomorrah. Isaiah 13, beginning with verse 19: "And Babylon, the glory of kingdoms, the beauty of the Chaldees' excellency, shall be as when God overthrew Sodom and Gomorrah. It shall never be inhabited, neither shall it be dwelt in from generation to generation: neither shall the Arabian pitch tent there; neither shall the shepherds make their fold there. But wild beasts and desert shall lie there; and their houses shall be full of doleful creatures; and owls shall dwell there, and satyrs shall dance there. And the wild beasts of the islands shall cry in their desolate houses, and dragons in their pleasant palaces; and her time is near to come, and her days shall not be prolonged." So, again the picture is of destruction that is complete, and that is permanent, that is irreversible.

And that's the future that awaits this present world system; we believe it may come in the very near future. The United States Secretary of Defense said, about a week ago, that he thinks there's a high likelihood that Israel will try to take out Iran's nuclear facilities sometime between April and June of this year. Russia and China are both backing Iran, and have sold Iran missiles that are easily capable of reaching Israel. And even if those missiles don't have nuclear warheads on them, conventional warheads - bombs of the old-fashioned kind - can wreak havoc, particularly in a small country, which is what Israel is.

There was a long piece in yesterday's USA Today describing how difficult it was going to be for Israel to even get to Iran to drop any bombs, since we've now pulled out of Iraq, and the Israeli air force can't use that route, which is the most direct route, to reach Iran. So the flashpoint may be a lot closer than we like to think; and Obama, who commands the most powerful armed forces in the world, seems to have no clue what to do about it.

It's not easy to imagine the scene described here - none of us have ever seen a whole city burning down. When I was a kid, I lived the whole time in the same house, in Springfield, Kentucky, the town where Paul and I started Temple Church. My folks moved into the house when I was four years old, and I was 26 when we moved away. Right directly across the street from where I lived was a large tobacco warehouse - it took up half a block; and those years, every time I looked out the window of my room, I say that warehouse.

Then one night in January, 1958 - I was 12 years old - it was already dark, we'd just had supper - I looked out the window, and the roof of the warehouse was blazing up. It wasn't a particularly large blaze at first - but because those warehouses had no interior walls, once it caught fire, you usually couldn't put it out. We tried to call the fire department - while we were looking up the number, the fire truck came rushing down the street - but there wasn't a lot they could do. They did manage to keep it from setting other buildings on fire - but 2 hours later, the warehouse was just a pile of ashes - and it had always stood in that spot, as long as I could remember.

But I remember that night like it had been only yesterday - and that's how the merchants of Babylon must have felt as they stood watching Babylon burn down.

Let me say one more thing, and I'm done. As you all know, Sunday afternoon singer Whitney Houston died suddenly and unexpectedly - they're still trying to determine exactly what killed her. She first became famous in early 1986 by recording a song that went "Learning to love yourself is the greatest love of all." It's a song about self-reliance, believing in yourself, and the basic message is, if you try hard enough, you can pull yourself up by your own bootstraps.

At the graduation exercises that year, at Washington County High School, the senior class sang it - and then Jimmy Reed, the football coach, gave the commencement address, and urged the graduates to love themselves, and believe in themselves. Of course, being a public school, you couldn't mention that you might need God's help.

Until I heard them sing it at commencement, I'd never heard the song - but I didn't think loving yourself squared very well with what the New Testament teaches; so on my radio broadcast the next week, I said so, and quoted St. Augustine's lines about loving God, even to the despising of self. Well, the folks at the public school didn't like it very much, of course.

Ok, how did loving yourself, and depending only on yourself, and ignoring the fact that you might need God to help you out - how did that turn out for Whitney Houston? By all accounts, she was struggling with drug problems, and having lots of trouble dealing with the adversities of life - and she was only in her 40's, I think. Self reliance works fine, so long as you're wealthy and popular, and in good health. But when adversity comes, you need God to help you. To love yourself is not the greatest love of all, I don't care what the public schools are teaching kids - it's not so.

Even if the Lord delays His coming, we will all one day stand where Babylon stands, in our text. Troubles come suddenly and unexpectedly; they may take your money, and your health, and your friends, and your family, and your acquaintances. So you need something more solid than this present world to hold onto. Babylon's problem wasn't just that she was rich - the problem was that she'd abandoned God.

And if we abandon God in our own hearts and lives, we'll one day find ourselves in the same place as the merchants of Babylon whom we've been talking about - wringing our hands and saying "Alas, alas!" I've lost everything that I ever cared about. We sometimes sing a song, "O sometimes the shadows are deep, and rough seems the path to the goal; And sorrows, sometimes how they sweep Like tempests down over the soul; O then to the Rock let me fly, to the Rock that is higher than I." And that's what we all need - it's what the merchants of Babylon needed, and didn't have.

Well, I'm going to leave it at that. Next week, we'll talk about the shipmasters - and we're coming down to the end of the chapter - I don't know whether we'll get it finished next week or not - but you all need to be back, and we'll take it up in verse 17.

Rev. 18:9-19

Tonight we return to the 18th chapter of Revelation. You'll recall that in the past weeks we've seem that chapters 17 and 18 pf Revelation are a unit, and they describe the fall of Babylon - which I told you, represents the ungodly world system - cultural, educational, political, economic. the chapter has five sections: (1) An angel announces the fall of Babylon, and gives the reasons for her fall - verses 1-3; (2) The angel warns God's people to come out of her, and to assist in her destruction - verses 4-8; (3) There is great mourning and lamentation by those who have been enjoying her sinful pleasures, and who have been enriched by her profits - verses 9-19, which is the longest section of the chapter, and the section at which we have now arrived; (4) God's people are invited to rejoice at her fall - verse 20; and (5) Babylon's final destruction is described - verses 21-24. As I say, we've now reached the third section, which is the longest - it runs for eleven verses - and it's a dirge, lament, over the fall of Babylon. Three groups are said to lament her fall - the kings, the merchants, and the ship owners and sailors. We've now talked about the lament of the kings, and the lament of the merchants. In verses 12 and 13, we saw a list of 29 items - and they're all luxury goods - not the type of things poor folks like us would have had - none of those John was writing to actually owned any of the things listed. And I tried to hit the high points of the things named in the lost of

"Preacher, why don't you get off this negative stuff? Why don't you preach something uplifting, like they do down at the prosperity gospel church?"

One answer is, because there's an awful lot of such negative stuff - condemnation of sin, and prophecies of doom there's an awful lot of it in the Scriptures - and if we only preach positive things, we've skipping over a large portion of the Bible.

Anyhow, getting back to Revelation, the verses before us, verses 17-19 of chapter 18, describe the dirge, the lament, of the seafaring men. They're described by four terms, verse 17, the last part of the verse: "And every shipmaster, and all of the company in ships, and sailors, and as many as trade by sea," I'd always been just reading past these four terms, and assuming they were all synonyms, that it was four ways of saying the same thing. But I'm learning something from this Bible study, whether anybody else is, or not. Every single word's important - we believe in the word-by-word inspiration of the Bible - and these words describe four different, disparate groups.

First of all, it mentions "shipmasters" - you might suppose that meant the guy who owned the ship, or perhaps the captain of the ship- but such is not the case. The word has a very precise meaning - it occurs only one other time in the New Testament, and only three times in the Old Testament, all three being in the 27th chapter of Ezekiel, where we were just reading - and it means the pilot, of helmsman, or steersman - the one who was physically guiding the ship through the water.

And if you think they're not important, think about the recent shipwreck in Italy. The captain decided he'd steer the ship himself, and he didn't know what he was doing, and he ran it into a rock, and the ship capsized. Does that remind you of some of these politicians who're trying to steer the ship of state, and seem to have no clue what they're doing?

The second group that's mentioned is "all the company in ships," and that's a different group. This is a sot where the various manuscripts differ - the difference is, essentially, whether the little word "the" should be there or not. One way of reading it, and the one the King James translators have adopted, is that it refers to the passengers on the ship. The other reading, which Dr. A. T. Robertson favors, and which seems to be the more likely meaning, is that it denotes sailors who only sail along the coast of the Mediterranean, never venturing out of sight of land.

That day in time, the magnetic compass hadn't yet been invented, so the only way you could navigate was by the start - which didn't work if it were cloudy, of course. So you had to either stay in sight of land, or else take your chances in he open sea, far from land, and hope you could tell where you were going. the alternate reading, which I've suggested, would have John saying that both classes of sailors - those who ventured into the open sea, and those who hugged the coastline, both were in the group mourning Babylon's fall. to those of us here several hundred miles from the ocean, it may seem like a find point but John was imprisoned on a small island, and he saw ships go by every single day. He had, obviously, been brought to Patmos on a ship, and if he were to ever get back o the seven churches he was writing to, he'd have o go by ship. So he knew about the different kinds of ships, just like we know about different kinds of cars.

Why should we care? I bring up that fine point for a couple of reasons. One is, to show how relatively insignificant the disputed readings in the Biblical text are, The liberals and the atheists say, "You can' trust the Bible - we can't be sure exactly what it says." I've had people tell me that. And in these fifty chapters of the Bible we've gone through verse by verse, we've not found more than three or four disputed readings - and none of than have concerned anything that was vital to our faith - no major doctrine is affected. It's interesting to know exactly what the word means - but it's not any reason to throw out your Bible, because you say, "It may have an error in it."

And the other reason I bring it up is this - this is a genuinely disputed passage - and none of the new translations catch it. They all translate it the same way the King James Version translates it. The New American Standard does have a footnote that says, "the alternate reading is: " But that's the nearest any of them comes to even acknowledging that there is a variant reading possible. These new translations aren't scholarly works. The guys putting them ut aren't really scholars - they're book salesmen. They're not concerned about getting it right - they've only concerned about making a lot of money.

War I - my dad could remember it - and everyone who lived through it, could remember where he was and what he was doing, when the news came that Germany had surrendered. There was similar rejoicing when World War II ended - he day Japan surrendered - they called it VJ Day. I was six weeks old; but all those who were older than I, well remembered VJ Day, and how they celebrated the day Japan surrendered.

This verse says there's going to be a similar celebration in heaven the day Satan is defeated. Dr. Clarke says: "the fall of this bad city was cause of grief to bad men. But as this city was a persecutor of the godly, and an enemy to the works of God, angels, apostles, and prophets are called to rejoice over her fall."

Dr. Barnes, similarly, writes: "They are commanded to rejoice over her ruin. There is a strong contrast between this language and what precedes. Kings, merchants, and seamen, who had been countenanced and sustained by her, would have occasion to mourn. But not so they who had been persecuted by her. Not so the church of the redeemed. Not so heaven itself. The great oppressor of the church and the corrupter of the world was now destroyed, and all the holy in heaven and on earth would have occasion to rejoice. this is not he language of vengeance, but it is the language of exultation and rejoicing.

Well, maybe. This presents the question - I've mentioned it before, and we'll be dealing with it throughout the next verses in this and the following chapter. How is this to be reconciled with the command that Christians should love their enemies, and pray for them? It's one of the difficulties, in understanding the book of Revelation, and it's one reason a lot of preachers and churches skip over it and never preach on it.

But I'll forego discussing it until next week. We'll take it up with verse 20; so go home, study the rest of this chapter, and then come back next week, when we'll resume our consideration of this chapter.

Rev. 18:20

Tonight we return to the 18th chapter of Revelation. You know by not that these two chapters, chapters 17 and 18, are a single unit, and concern the fall of Babylon – which we've identified as the entire corrupt world system. In verses 9-19, we see three groups mourning over the destruction of Babylon, namely, the kings, the merchants, and the mariners. Last week we considered the third of these groups, the sailors and ship owners, which is set out in verses 17-19.

I noted that it's quite similar to a dirge that Ezekiel pronounced over Tyre, in the 27th chapter of his prophecy. I argued that this similarity is a proof of the divine inspiration of Scripture, since John obviously didn't have a copy of Ezekiel with him on Patmos; and I also commented that this passage in Ezekiel, like many passages in the Bible, is one that no one ever preaches on.

We talked about exactly which groups are meant by the terms John uses. By "shipmasters" - the Greek word is *kubernetes* - he means the steersmen – the ones who actually guided the boat through the water; by "all the company in ships" - in Greek it's only three words, not five as we have in English - its *homilos*, meaning, "a crowd of men gathered together" - it's the only time this particular word occurs in the New Testament - *homilos epi* - proposition, means "on" - *homlios epi ploion* - which means ship - so he's talking about the passengers on the ships; and then *nautes* - think about our English word "nautical" - he's talking about the sailors, who would now be out of work because of Babylon's fall; and we talked about the difference between sailors who only sailed along the coastline, and never got out of sight of land; and those who sailed in the open sea, far from land.

I also commented that the sailors, like the merchants, are mourning over the wrong thing – they're not mourning over their sins – they're only mourning because those sins have caught up with them. Paul said that 'Godly sorrow leadeth to repentance," but theirs was not Godly sorrow – it was the sorrow of the world, which, Paul adds, worketh death.

Then we came on to verse 20, and noted that this verse calls upon God's people to rejoice over the fall of Babylon. I contrasted this with the rejoicing by Satan's crowd when the two witnesses were slain, chapter 11 of Revelation, and used the term that now, it was "payback time." I compared it to the rejoicing at the end of World War I, when Germany surrendered, or on VJ Day in 1945 when the Japanese surrendered at the end of World War II.

As we closed, I brought up the question, which we've mentioned before, of how this command to rejoice over the fall of the wicked, is to be reconciled with the words of Jesus that we should love our enemies. I deferred discussion of that point until this week, and said that this question will remain a part of our discussion, for several weeks, until we get through chapters 18 and 19.

Anyhow, that was last week. Now, taking it up there, we have a bit more to say about verse 20, before we go on to verses 21-24. Verse 20: "Rejoice over her, thou heaven, and ye holy apostles and prophets; for God hath avenged you on her." As I noted last week, this is a command - it's in the imperative mood - and it's followed by a description of her destruction, in verses 21-24 of this chapter; and then, immediately following her destruction, in chapter 19, vs. 1, heaven erupts with a mighty roar of a great multitude in heaven shouting praise to God that He has condemned the great whore and avenged the blood of His servants. Dr. A.T. Robertson refers to this as "the song of doom."

This call for God's people to rejoice over their enemies, is reminiscent of a passage in the Old Testament. You may recall that the Book of Deuteronomy sets out Moses's final message to the children of Israel, whom he has led for 40 years. It ends with something called "The Song of Moses," and the song of Moses ends with these words - Deut. 32:43: "Rejoice, O ye nations, with his people: for he will avenge the blood of his servants, and will render vengeance to his adversaries, and will be merciful unto his land, and to his people." If this is an obscure passage to us, it would not have been obscure to John and the other Jewish believers. To them, the song of Moses was a very important passage - and it should be to us, since we're told that in heaven we'll sing "the song of Moses and of the lamb"; and the song of Moses ends with a cry for vengeance.

As I indicated when we closed last week, this question of how you reconcile the calls for vengeance with the teaching about loving your enemies, is a question that is central to the consideration of these chapters, and we'll be coming back to it again. I did not say, that we will resolve the difficulty; but we will discuss it, and try to shed what light we can on this troubling aspect of Revelation.

Those who are admonished, commanded to rejoice, are: "thou heaven, and ye holy apostles and prophets." I take "ye heaven" to mean "the inhabitants of heaven" - those who dwell in heaven - which would include God, and the angels, and the four living creatures, and the glorified saints. But this indicates that those in heaven are interested on what's going on, on the earth. Hebrews 12:1 says: Wherefore, seeing we also are compassed about with so great a cloud of witnesses, let us lay aside every weight, and the sin which doth so easily beset us, and run with patience the race that is set before us." We've all got friends and loved ones who are in heaven - and these verses indicate that, not only is God watching our race and our walk here, but those who have preceded us to heaven, are also watching our battle with Satan, and cheering us on.

Incidentally, those in hell are also interested in what's going on on the earth - because in Luke 16, the rich man says to Lazarus: "I pray thee therefore, father, that thou wouldst send him to my father's house: For I have five brethren, that he may testify unto them, lest they also come into this place of torment." I remember one time hearing G. Christian Weiss preaching on Back to the Bible Broadcast, about the call to missions. He had four points - he said the call to witness comes from within, as the Holy Ghost calls us; from without, because our concern for the welfare of the lost should cause us to witness to them; it comes from above, because God has commanded us to go and witness; but it also comes from below, and he read this passage from Luke, chapter 16 and verses 27 and 28.

And then it says: "ye holy apostles." The word "apostle" only occurs three times in the book of Revelation - back in chapter two, where he says, "thou hast tried them that say they are apostles, and are not." The term occurs in chapter 21, where it says that in the foundations of the New Jerusalem, are the names of "the twelve apostles of the Lamb." And then, of course, it occurs here, in chapter 18, verse 20. The term "apostles" usually refers to the twelve; but occasionally in the New Testament it is used to refer to others. Barnabas is called an apostle in Acts 14:14, for example. But without taking the time to discuss whether the New Testament is always consistent in its use of the term, it's pretty clear that here, it means the twelve, since in Chapter 21, verse 14, it speaks of the twelve foundations having in them "the names of the twelve apostles of the Lamb."

The term - the Greek word is apostoloi - means, basically, "one who is sent." The term first occurs in Matthew 10:2, where Jesus is sending them forth to preach in Israel; prior to that time, they're simply called His "disciples," which is a different term, and denotes those who are being taught, being instructed. The term "apostle" can mean an ambassador, or a delegate, or a messenger. But it clearly carries the idea of one who is called out, set apart, and sent. And this idea is emphasized by the fact that, here, they're called the "holy apostles."

Incidentally, many manuscripts have the word "and" between "holy" and "apostles," so that it would read "thou heaven, and ye saints and apostles and prophets." Most of the other versions have gone with that reading, as seeming the more likely - it doesn't materially affect the meaning of the verse. But the word translated "holy" is *hagioi*. It occurs frequently in Revelation, and also in the rest of the Bible. Thayer's Greek treatise defines *hagioi* this way: "Its fundamental idea is separation, consecration and devotion to the service of God. It implies that what is set apart from the world and to God, should separate itself from the world's defilements, and should share in God's purity."

God tells the children of Israel, Lev. 19:2: "Ye shall be holy, for I the Lord your God am holy." And in I Peter 2:9, we're told that Christians are "an holy nation" and "a peculiar people." It means, the commentator says, that "the children of Israel are not merely God's inheritance, but that they must separate themselves from abominations of the heathen nations around them." The commentator adds that "One side of this holiness is its intolerance of unholiness and active war against it."

We talked Sunday morning in Sunday school about Joseph fleeing from Potiphar's wife when she tried to entice him. That's what all Christians should do - flee from evil. Not far from where John was, on the mainland of Greece, was a temple to the god Aesculapius. Inscribed over the entrance of the temple were the words: "H who would enter the divine temple must be pure; and purity is to have a mind which thinks holy thoughts."

I've spoken before, frequently, about the importance of Christian separation - which sets us apart from most churches, that never mention it. Pentecostal churches used to make a big point of preaching separation - that's why they were called "holiness" churches - because they stressed holy living. But you don't hear much about it in most churches today. Perhaps you think I'm hitting this point too often. My response is, we're going through Genesis on Sunday morning and through Revelation on Wednesday night, a verse at a time - and I've placed no more emphasis, and no less emphasis, on separation, than the Bible does. The reason I keep bringing it back up is because the Bible does - it's taught throughout the parallel testaments.

And then it speaks of the "prophets." A prophet is one who foretells, but also one who "forth tells." The gift of prophecy is one of the spiritual gifts mentioned in the New Testament; but the reference here may be primarily to the Old Testament prophets. Jesus said, Luke 11, verse 49: "Therefore also said the wisdom of God, I will send them prophets and apostles, and some of them they shall slay and persecute." John was standing there, of course, and heard Him say it.

And so now, when we get on down to the last verse of this chapter, verse 24, he says, referring to Babylon: "And in her was found the blood of prophets, and of saints, and of all that were slain upon the earth." And in the previous chapter, chapter 17, when John first sees Babylon, it says: "And I saw the woman drunken with the blood of the saints, and with the blood of the martyrs of Jesus." And, of course, in the Sermon on the Mount, Jesus told the disciples that when they persecute you: "Rejoice, and be exceeding glad: for great is your reward in heaven: for so persecuted they the prophets which were before you."

Folks like to talk about the Sermon on the Mount - and they'll tell you that it says, "Love your enemies" - and it does. They'll tell you that it says: "Judge not, that ye be not judged" - and it most certainly does. But do they ever tell you about the verse I just read - Matt. 5:12 - that if you live for God, you're going to be persecuted? Uh-uh; when it comes to that part, the liberal churches fall strangely silent. They only want to talk about the things in the Sermon on the Mount, that they agree with.

And then we come to this troubling last phrase of the verse: "for God hath avenged you on her." How are we to deal with that? As I said last week, the way most churches deal with it is to ignore it, and pretend it's not in there. We'll try and do a little better than that.

In the first place, the original Greek has a play on words that doesn't come across in English. Most people have been taught to think that learning and civilization began with Sponge Bob and Dolly Parton, and that all the folks back in John's time were ignorant, stupid, uneducated. It's not so - the things they wrote - and particularly what God inspired them to write - the language is very carefully constructed.

In this particular instance, the word in question is *krino,* which means "to judge." Our word "criticize" comes from that Greek word. And what it literally says is, "God has judged your judgment." The word *krino* is there in both its noun and verb forms. The Greek word "judgment" can have two meanings; one is, what a judge does in court. He sits behind the judicial bench, and decides the case - and what he issues is called a "judgment." But it can also mean the sentence imposed for a crime. You send someone up for twenty years; or you execute him - that's "judgment" - the state makes him pay for his crime.

In chapter 17, verse 1, John is told: "Come hither; I will shew unto thee the judgment of the great whore." Now, in that verse, it means, "I'll show you her punishment" - the execution of the sentence against her. But in the verse before us, verse 20 of chapter 18, it means an adjudication; God as a judge, sitting in judgment. That's something his readers would have known about - they were being persecuted, and Caesar was using the judicial machinery of the state to persecute them. Just as Obama's trying to do to Christians, for example.

And John, who had himself been sentenced to exile by some judicial tribunal, is saying to his fellow believers, "Caesar's judgment against you, against me, isn't the last word. There's a higher court; and in that superior tribunal in heaven, God has already ruled in our favor. God has treated her the same way she treated His people."

We've already seen this in verse 6: "Reward her even as she rewarded you." In other words, give back to her as she has given to you. In Galatians 6:7, we're told: "Whatsoever a man soweth, that shall he also reap." That's the principal that's operating here - Babylon is reaping what she sowed.

Dr. Barnes paraphrases it: "God has taken vengeance on her for her treatment of you. That is, as Babylon had persecuted the church, all those in heaven are interested in it, and affected by it. All the redeemed, therefore, in earth and in heaven, are interested in whatever tends to retard or to promote the cause of truth. All have occasion to mourn when the enemies of the truth triumph; to rejoice when they fall." In other words, those in heaven are interested in the outcome of this coming election, and they will rejoice when Obama leaves office next January - if he does.

Back in chapter 6, you may remember that when the fifth seal was opened, John says, chapter 6 and verse 9: "And when he had opened the fifth seal, I saw under the altar the souls of them that were slain for the word of God, and for the testimony which they held: And they cried with a loud voice, saying, How long, O Lord holy and true, dost thou not judge and avenge our blood on them that dwell on the earth?"

And you know how the text goes. They're told: "that they should rest yet for a little season, until their fellow-servants also and their brethren that should be killed as they were, should be fulfilled." Seven years have now passed, and now, at last, the cry of the martyrs is about to be answered. Their waiting has come to an end; and they are told to rejoice that God has avenged them.

There's another verse along that line. In the 18th chapter of Luke's gospel, we're told about an unjust judge - He could have been describing some of the one's I've known - He could have been describing the seven Supreme Court justices who decided *Roe v. Wade* - whom I refer to as the seven greatest mass murderers in human history. And Jesus's application of the story is, Luke 18, verse 7-8: "And shall not God avenge his own elect, which cry day and night unto him, though he bear long with them? I tell you that he will avenge them speedily." John was standing there, and heard Him speak those words. Now, sixty years later, he's given a vision of that avengement Jesus promised, finally coming to pass.

But, of course, we've still not answered the underlying question, that I raised at the beginning of the hour; namely, how is this to be reconciled with the command that we love our enemies? And, friends, there's an awful lot of language in the Bible that talks about vengeance - you can only preach a gospel that God is a god of all love, by ignoring large passages of the Bible - which is what most preachers and churches are content to do.

One possible answer, and the one which is available to us as premillenialists, as dispensationalists, is that we're in the dispensation of grace; and at the time John's talking about, the dispensation of grace is over, and the time of judgment has begun. Let me read you a couple of sentences that commentator Ethelbert Bullinger wrote about 140 years ago: "Some commentators apologize for this rejoicing in vengeance; and endeavor to tone it down, as being inconsistent with the Gospel. Of course it is inconsistent with the Gospel; but this is because the dispensations are not the same. Once rightly divide the word of truth, and all difficulty is removed."

Well, maybe. We'll return to this question again, as we go through the next couple of chapters. Let me make a couple of more comments, and we'll close. In the Sermon on the Mount, Jesus said, "Love your enemies." And all of the other similar admonitions in the New Testament are similarly directed - "If thine enemy hunger, feed him; and if he thirst, give him drink." We're told to love our enemies. On the other hand, we are never told to love God's enemies. Quite the contrary; in Psalm 139, verses 20 and 21, we read: "Do not I hate them, O Lord, that hate thee? and am I not grieved with those that rise up against thee? I hate them with perfect hatred: I count them mine enemies."

Those words, in Psalm 139:22, are followed immediately by verse 23, which is more familiar to us, and reads: "Search me, O God, and know my heart: try me, and know my thoughts: and see if there be any wicked way in me, and lead me in the way everlasting." We're accustomed to reading those last two verses, without any consideration for the two verses immediately preceding. Reading the full passage, it seems to imply that the sin David was worried about, was that he hadn't hated God's enemies thoroughly enough. And I'd be willing to wager that you'd have to look long and hard to find any on he other church on the road, that has ever preached on Psalm 139, verses 20 and 21.

And finally, I've got one other observation on this point. We're accustomed to think of the Bible, and the gospel message, as concerned only with individual salvation. So we're told to, stay out of politics, and just concentrate on getting men saved. Now, I'm as devoted to personal evangelism, getting men saved, as anybody. I've been doing it for more than fifty years.

But, having said that, these chapters aren't just about individual salvation. It's clear that the whole society was shot through with corruption. These chapters talk about personal salvation - because chapter 17, verse 8, talks about those whose names are written in the Lamb's book of life. But these chapters also talk about economic activity - trade and commerce - that's why we read about merchants and ship masters. It's also about politics, because we read about the kings, bewailing the loss of their power.

And I sincerely believe that we are not preaching the whole counsel of God, if we fail to point out the sins of our nation's leaders - the President, the congress, the Supreme Court, as well as the administrative agencies which seem increasingly to be running everybody's lives. Churches need to take a stand on the question of abortion, instead of hiding behind the excuse that, "We believe in the separation of church and state, so we can't talk about that."

I've said before, and make no apology for repeating, that there are a lot of people in Washington, and elsewhere, who want to limit the First Amendment guarantee of freedom of religion, limit it to what goes out over the pulpit on Sunday morning. They want us to believe, the First Amendment doesn't apply to what they teach in the public schools five days a week, six hours a day. Rick Santorum was on Glenn Beck's show last Thursday, and he said that, quote: "62% of kids who go into college with a faith commitment leave without it." Shouldn't that concern us as churches? And you know that the vast majority of the kids he's talking about go to public, government-run colleges.

Lifeway, which is the Southern Baptist publishing house, did a survey in 2007. They found that seven in 10 Protestants ages 18 to 30 who went to church regularly in high school said they quit attending by age 23. That survey was taken five years ago - do you think things have gotten any better since then? Or have they gotten even worse?

A guy named William D'Antonio, who teaches at the Catholic University of America in Washington, D.C., made a survey of Roman Catholics. Between 1993 and 2011, a period of eighteen years, the percentage of Catholics who said they were "highly committed" to their religious faith, fell from 27% in 1993, to 19% in

2011. Dr. D'Antonio's explanation for why it happened was, "blame mortality. The most highly committed Catholics are seniors and they're dying out." Is that true? What about Baptist churches? I say, look around you - how many folks under 30 years of age do we have here on the average Sunday morning?

Preacher, where are you getting all this stuff from? It was in USA Today, the day before yesterday - Monday morning. So I believe there is cause for grave concern, and churches need to wake up and realize what's going on.

Well, I'm going to leave it there. We've gotten through verse 20 - so we'll take it up with verse 21 next Wednesday night.

Rev.18:21-24

Tonight we return to the 18th chapter of Revelation. You know by now that these two chapters, chapters 17 and 18, are a single unit, and concern the fall of Babylon – which we've identified as the entire corrupt world system. In verses 9-19, we see three groups mourning over the destruction of Babylon, namely, the kings, the merchants, and the mariners. Last week we considered verse 20: "Rejoice over her, thou heaven, and ye holy apostles and prophets; for God hath avenged you on her."

As I noted last week, this is a command - it's in the imperative mood - and it's followed by a description of her destruction, in verses 21-24 of this chapter; and then, immediately following her destruction, in chapter 19, vs. 1, heaven erupts with a mighty roar of a great multitude in heaven shouting praise to God that He has condemned the great whore and avenged the blood of His servants. I noted that verse 20 is similar to Deut. 32:43, the closing verse of the Song of Moses: "Rejoice, O ye nations, with his people: for he will avenge the blood of his servants, and will render vengeance to his adversaries, and will be merciful unto his land, and to his people."

And I pointed out that, when Moses came to end his 40 years of ministry to the Israelites, he closed his farewell sermon with a call for vengeance - which is not a point that you'll hear very often - but it's clearly what the text says. Now, as we're nearing the end of the book of Revelation, John echoes a similar theme. We also discussed, as we had the previous week, the conundrum, the puzzle, of how you reconcile what the Bible says about the love of God, with the calls for vengeance, both here and elsewhere. I suggested that one possible solution is to say, these words were all written in a different dispensation. And I'll have a bit more to say on that point, during the course of my remarks this evening.

We noted that four groups are called upon to rejoice over Babylon's fall: (1) "thou heaven", meaning those in heaven - God, the angels, the glorified saints; (2) "ye holy", meaning the saints who are still on earth; (3) "ye apostles", meaning the twelve, of whom John was the last one left alive, of course; and (4) "and prophets," and we talked about the function of prophets, in both the Old Testament, and in the New Testament.

We also discussed the two different meanings of the word "judgment," as it's used in this chapter. It can mean the adjudication itself - the judge - God, in this case - the judge sitting behind the judicial bench and pronouncing judgment. And it can also mean the execution of the sentence, the imposition of punishment.

Well, anyhow, that brings us to the fifth section of this chapter - verses 21-24, that describes the destruction of Babylon - which, I've insisted, symbolizes the entire corrupt, Satanic world system - economic, political, cultural, religious. These verses present a sharp contrast to verse 20 - in verses 11-19, we've seen the kings and the merchants weeping and wailing over Babylon's fall. Then in verse 20, we see the saints in heaven rejoicing over Babylon's fall; but here in the next verse, verse 21, the somber note resumes, and continues to the end of the chapter, verse 24. But then in the following verse, the first verse of chapter 19, we again see the rejoicing in heaven. So these chapters are a study in contrasts - remember what I've told you about the two antiphonal choirs, answering back and forth?

The chapter also contrasts the end of Babylon's music, with the heavenly music which is mentioned repeatedly throughout the book; the light of a candle will no longer shine in Babylon, contrasted with the city of heaven where they need no light of a candle, because the Lord God giveth them light; the voices of bridegroom and bride will no longer be heard in heaven, by contrast with God's saints, who have gone in to the marriage supper of the Lamb.

Now look with me at verse 21: "And a mighty angel took up a stone like a great millstone, and cast it into the sea, saying, Thus with violence shall that great city Babylon be thrown down, and shall be found no more at all.". This is a verse about a rock - a stone. It says the stone was "like a great millstone," which may mean that "it appeared to be a millstone" or, perhaps, "about the same size as a millstone." I don't know exactly how much the millstones they used in Palestine at that time weighed; but you can actually order them on line. You can get one that's 6 feet in diameter, 2 ½ feet thick, and weighs 10,600 lbs. - more than five tons - it costs $3800.00. You can get a lot of things on line. So if it were a millstone that size, it would have required "a mighty angel" to lift it and toss it around.

My great-grandfather owned a mill, in Springfield; my great-great grandfather owned one in Mitchellsburg, Kentucky, which was near Danville, Bro. Paul. And that day in time - nearly 150 years ago - it made you an important person in the community. In pioneer times, most folks were pretty self-sufficient. They raised their own food, chopped their own firewood, made their own clothes; but the one thing they couldn't do on the farm was to grind their own flour or meal. Building a mill was a big enough expense, that each town only had one; it was one of the few things you actually had to go into town for, was to get your corn, or your wheat, ground. And so the mill was usually the biggest business in town. If you've ever visited a place called Cades Cove, in the Great Smoky Mountains, they actually have an operating grist mill, with a water wheel turning the millstones.

You'll notice that it's referred to as a "great millstone." No word is accidental, every word has a reason for being there; and in this case, it's to distinguish the kind of millstone you'd have in a grist mill, from a handmill, like you might have at home. You've surely seen pictures depicting women grinding meal on a small mill at home - that's the kind of mill it refers to when it says: "two shall be grinding at the mill; one shall be taken, and the other left," when the rapture comes. They only weighed a hundred pounds or so. John wanted his readers to understand that he wasn't talking about on of these hundred pound jobs - it was a "great millstone," one like you'd find at a grist mill, that might weigh half a ton.

Now, the angel doesn't just drop it into the sea; although, something that weighed that much, simply dropping it would have been quite sufficient, particularly if you were dropping it a considerable distance - we don't know exactly how high above the sea the angel dropped it from - but the farther it falls, the faster it goes; so by the time it hit the water, if would have been going fairly fast, just from the force of gravity. But the angel doesn't just drop it - he hurls it into the sea. When he says, "Thus with violence shall Babylon be thrown down," the Greek word translated "violence," - *hormema* - it literally means, "with a rush." It's the only time that particular word occurs in the New Testament, by the way.

I'll digress long enough to say that this is, clearly, a spot where you actually could make the King James language a little clearer, make the meaning a bit more precise. None of the new versions do - not a single one - they all use the same word as the King James does - "violence" - so much for the claim that the new versions are scholarly works, or that they make the meaning a lot clearer. Here's one place where they actually could - and not a one of them does. The guys hawking these things aren't scholars - they're slick talking book salesmen, whom Satan's sent out to confuse people; and you can tell the liberal preachers that I said so.

Dr. A. T. Robertson paraphrases it "like a boulder hurled into the sea." That gives you the sense of what he's talking about. And as John watched the millstone sinking into the sea, he may have thought of what Moses said, after the Red Sea had covered Pharoah's chariots, and his horsemen, and his army, Ex. 15:5: "The depths have covered them; they sank into the bottom as a stone."

Or perhaps he thought of how Nehemiah described it, looking back on the event more than a thousand years later, Neh. 9:11: "And thou didst divide the sea before them, so that they went through the midst of the sea on the dry land; and their persecutors thou threwst into the deeps, as a stone into the mighty waters."

Or perhaps he thought of the words of Jeremiah. Jeremiah prophesied many years, lived to see his prophecy fulfilled, the city of Jerusalem fall, and the people carried off into captivity. His prophecy runs on for 51 chapters; and he ended his prophecy with these words - chapter 51, verses 63 and 64: "And it shall be, when thou hast made an end of reading this book, that thou shalt bind a stone to it, and cast it into the midst of Euphrates: And thou shalt say, Thus shall Babylon sink, and shall not rise from the evil that I will bring up: and they shall be weary. Thus far are the words of Jeremiah."

Now, did you know that was in there? I didn't - I'm learning something, whether anybody else is or not. If somebody had asked me, "What did Jeremiah do with his prophecy when he'd finished writing it?" I wouldn't have known - and I certainly wouldn't have said, "He threw it in the creek." But the passage may have been more familiar to John than it is to us - we've seen repeatedly in these last two chapters that John refers to things that are written in Jeremiah.

So verse 21 speaks of a "great stone"; and in these two chapters, John has repeatedly referred to Babylon as "that great city" - he says it seven different times, in these two chapters. So the "great stone" symbolizes the "great city," and his meaning is that, at the last. Babylon is going to sink like a rock; she's going to be as completely gone, as a rock covered by the sea. As we've seen, Babylon represents this entire corrupt world system - culture, government, false religion, education - what's its destiny? What shall be the end of these things? The Bible's answer is, the whole ungodly mess is going to sink like a rock, and disappear forever.

Is that what they're going to tell you down at the prosperity gospel church? Probably not - but that's what John wrote; and that's why people don't preach on Revelation. It's not because they can't understand what it says - quite the contrary - they understand it all too well - it says that, any day now, they're going to be out of business, permanently - so they skip over it and say, "Don't read Revelation; it'll just confuse you." What they really mean is, "We don't want you to know what it says."

Next month, on the 12th of April, to be exact, will be the 100th anniversary of the sinking of the Titanic. One moment, the 1300 passengers were sailing along securely on their way to America - and then a couple of hours later - 160 minutes later, if you want to be exact - the ship was at the bottom of the Atlantic Ocean. About ten years ago, some divers, treasure hunters, actually located it at the bottom of the ocean. That's similar to what's going to happen to Babylon, to this world system - except in this case, it's not going to be rediscovered in 90 years - or ever. Babylon's disappearance will be sudden, and it will be permanent - like a huge stone sinking into the ocean.

Many civilizations suffer a gradual decline - things run downhill, over a long period of time. Rome did, Gibbon's history of the decline and fall of Rome describes its having occurred over a period of more than 1300 years. The collapse described here isn't gradual - it's sudden. Four times is says "in one day" or "in one hour."

Moreover, as I've already noted, the stone doesn't simply fall of its own weight - it's hurled violently into the ocean - with added impetus provided by an outside force. So the final collapse of society won't be simply by its deterioration; it's not going to fall of its own weight - God's going to give it a shove. Which agrees entirely with what the Bible says in II Thess. 2:11, where he's describing the coming of Antichrist, Paul writes: "And for this cause God shall send them strong delusion, that they should believe a lie." The stone, meaning the world system, doesn't simply fall of its own weight - the angel gives it a sling, to accelerate its fall.

And then, not only will Babylon's fall be sudden, and complete; but it will also be permanent. I've already referred to the prophecy of Jeremiah. In chapter 7 of Jeremiah, verse 34, Jeremiah makes a similar prediction concerning Jerusalem: "Then will I cause to cease from the cities of Judah and from the streets of Jerusalem, the voice of mirth, and the voice of gladness, the voice of the bridegroom, and the voice of the bride: for the land shall be desolate."

This prophecy was given fairly early in Jeremiah's ministry; and he lived to see its fulfillment, when Nebuchadnezzar conquered Jerusalem, and carried the people off captive to Babylon. But, in that case, God also told Jeremiah to predict Judah's restoration - chapter 33, verses 10 and 11: "Thus saith the Lord, Again there shall be heard in this place, which ye say shall be desolate without man and without beast, even in the cities of Judah, and in the streets of Jerusalem, that are desolate, without man, and without inhabitant, and without beast, The voice of joy, and the voice of gladness, the voice of the bridegroom, and the voice of the bride, the voice of them that shall say, Praise the Lord of hosts: for the Lord is good; for his mercy endureth for ever: and of them that shall bring the sacrifice of praise into the house of the Lord. For I will cause to return the captivity of the land, as at the first, saith the Lord."

Incidentally, if you read the beginning of that chapter, chapter 33 of Jeremiah, you'll notice that Jeremiah was in prison when he found any more in thee; and the sound of a millstone shall be heard no more at all in thee; And the light of a candle shall shine no more at all in thee; and the voice of the bridegroom and of the bride shall be heard no more at all in thee: for thy merchants were the great men of the earth; for by thy sorceries were all nations deceived."

You'll note the phrase "no more" is repeated six times, identifying six specific things that it says will no longer take place in Babylon. But I think we'll stop there, and leave those verses for next week, when hopefully we'll manage to finish the chapter.

If you think I'm repeating myself - preacher, isn't this pretty much the same thing that it said in verses 11-19? The answer is "Yes," but the reason I'm hitting the points again, is because John does. God wanted to be sure we got the point; and, as we've done for the past five years now, we're taking it verse by verse, and trying not to leave out anything, but be sure we give the material a careful and a thorough treatment.

So go home and read the rest of the chapter - there's only three more verses - and then come back next week and we'll discuss them, and try to finish the chapter, and then the following week, begin chapter 19, which sets out John's account of the Second Coming. It's taken us five years to get here, but we're finally getting to the "one far off, Divine event, toward which the whole creation moves." So you don't want to miss a single week - it's all extremely important.

Rev. 18:21-24

Tonight we return to the 18th chapter of Revelation, and we're nearing the end of this chapter, and of the vision about the destruction of Babylon, which is set out in Revelation, chapters 17 and 18. When we do, as I mentioned when we closed last week, the next chapter, chapter 19, sets out John's description of the Second Coming of our Lord. It's taken us more than five years to get there, but we're finally getting to the climax of the story, the high action of the drama, the final wind-up of the account.

As we've noted, this chapter is like two competing choirs, singing an anthem responsively - the technical term is *antiphonal,* which simply means, responsively. I say that because, in verses 9-19, we see Babylon's merchants, kings, and shipmasters, bewailing her fall - and it is poetic in form. Then in verse 20, we have those in heaven rejoicing over her fall; and then in tonight's text, verses 21-24, again we have a reference to the destruction of Babylon - we'll get into that in a minute. And then, in the first few verses of chapter 19, we again see heaven rejoicing. Think, perhaps, of John standing somewhere removed from both, and glancing first at the chaos on earth, and then glancing upward, and beholding the joy in heaven.

Last week, we saw that there were four groups rejoicing over the fall of Babylon: "ye heavens," meaning those in heaven - God, the angels, the four beasts, the redeemed saints; "ye holy," meaning the saved who are still on earth - who rejoice because the time of their persecution has finally ended; the "apostles," meaning the twelve, of whom John was the last one remaining alive; and ""prophets", whom I take to be the Old Testament prophets. Jesus had said to the disciples, when they persecute you, remember that "so persecuted they the prophets which were before you."

This verse isn't a suggestion, or just an admonition; it's a command - it's in the imperative mood. The command to rejoice over the collapse of Babylon is just as much a command, as are the Ten Commandments. So we turned to the question of, "How can this language be reconciled with the commands in the Sermon on the Mount, and elsewhere in the New Testament, that we love our enemies?" I suggested that a lot of preachers and churches deal with the problem by simply ignoring it, and pretending those verses aren't in the Bible - and if anyone asks them, they reply, "Well, God didn't intend for us to understand that." I hold a different view, and assert that if God put it in the Bible, we have a duty to at least try to understand what it means. We'll never have perfect knowledge until we get to heaven - but we're supposed to at least try and figure it out, with the aid of the Holy Ghost.

I suggested that one possible explanation is, that this is a different dispensation, and we're now in the dispensation of grace. Now, that approach has some problems, and in the course of my remarks tonight, I'll suggest an alternative explanation. As I told you, this is one of the difficulties presented by the book of Revelation, and as we make our way through the book, we'll continue to encounter passages raising the question.

Anyway, that's what we covered last week. Now, tonight, we take up the last four verses of the chapter, verses 21-24. It seems, at first glance, repetitious of what we've just read in verses 9-19, where we saw the kings, and the merchants, and the mariners lamenting the fall of Babylon. I'm sure that a lot of preachers would say, "We've already discussed that," and skip over it. And the fact that I'm covering four verses in one night, when I frequently spend the whole time on a single verse, suggests that we have been over it already, and so we can get along a little faster. But God put it in the Bible, and I don't feel free to just disregard it.

Now, why'd God put some of the material in a second time? Perhaps, to make sure we got the point. In the school of education, they told us, "Repetition is the first law of learning." So God may have been following that philosophy. But I'd like to also suggest that these two sections present the matter from two different perspectives. Think of a photographer, taking a picture of the same structure, from two different perspectives - a front view, and a side view, for example. Or think of one photograph being made from across the street, and another photograph being made from a satellite.

In verses 9-19, we saw it from the perspective of the kings, merchants, and mariners. In our text, we see the same events, viewed from heaven's perspective. It's a little hard to find a good parallel, but think of the events of 9/11. From Alcaida's perspective, it was a great victory - remember that the Arab community in Milwaukee, got out in the streets and celebrated? As did the Palestinians in Israel, and in several of the Arab countries. But from our perspective, it was a tragedy, and an attack, and one to which we responded by sending our army to wipe them out. Same thing for the American Civil War - from the North's perspective, it was a great victory. From the South's perspective, it was a signal defeat. My great-grandmother had two brothers who fought in the Confederate army, and some us are still mad about it.

Now, you'll notice that in verses 21 and 22, the phrase "no more" recurs six times. Again, this section is poetic in form. And it implies two things - that the destruction he's describing is total, and that it's permanent. The harpers, and the musicians, and the craftsmen, and the others it lists, are all of them gone. God hasn't just reduced the number of nightclubs on earth - he's eliminated all of them - and they're never coming back. Most military victories aren't quite that complete. We defeated Japan - but Hirohito remained on the throne. We defeated Germany, Hitler killed himself; but Germany came back, and is now the strongest economic power in Europe. When God destroys Babylon, the destruction is going to be total, and it's going to be permanent. They're never coming back.

Now, what is it that's fixing to disappear? In a word, the entire corrupt world system - but some specific components of that world system are enumerated, as having been destroyed. First, it mentions "harpers, musicians, pipers, and trumpets". He's describing the entertainment industry - Hollywood, and all it stands for. Of course, they didn't have pianos, and they certainly didn't have electric organs, such as we have here in the sanctuary. We're told that David played a harp, and in Revelation, we've repeatedly read about the redeemed having harps in their hands. So there's a contrast - no more harps on earth, but harps in heaven.

Harp music wasn't usually played solo - the harpers usually accompanied singing - so the "harpers" and the "musicians," which evidently means "singers," go together. The pipers are playing an instrument that's something like the flutes we have today. Musical instruments have improved a bit through the years. It's questionable whether the music has.

And it mentions "trumpets." We've read about trumpets several times in the book of Revelation. When Jesus first appeared to John, in chapter one, John says that he heard a voice that sounded like a trumpet. And of course, we read in I Corinthians 15, "The trumpet shall sound, and the dead shall be raised incorruptible; and we shall all be changed." Similarly, in Thessalonians, we read that: "The Lord Himself shall descend from heaven with a shout, with the voice of the archangel, and with the trump of God; and the dead in Christ shall rise first."

In Israel, in the Old Testament, trumpets were used to summon the people to worship, or to battle, it was used to warn if there were an enemy approaching - but here, it seems to indicate the use of a trumpet for entertainment. When I was young, there was a famous black trumpet player named Louis Armstrong, who was quite popular.

So, the first four things mentioned here all relate to the entertainment industry. I hardly have to tell you that, in today's

America, entertainment has hit a new low, and is leading lots of people to hell. In 1955, Sword of the Lord published a book entitled, *Hollywood Cesspool*. And the movies made in 1955 seem tame compared to the ones they're making today. They didn't have movies in John's day, of course, but they did have stage plays.

A hundred years after John wrote Revelation, Clement of Alexandria, wrote: ""Let spectacles, therefore, and plays that are full of indecent language and abundant gossip be forbidden. For what base action is there that is not exhibited in the theaters?" About that same time, Tertullian wrote: "Are we not, in like manner, commanded to put away from us all immodesty? On this ground, again, we are excluded from the theater, which is immodesty's own particular abode. . . . The very harlots, too, victims of the public lust, are brought upon the stage. . . Is it right to look on what it is disgraceful to do?" That's the stuff John was objecting to; and the theater, movies, and television today, are a whole lot worse than what Clement and Tertullian were objecting to.

When John R. Rice published his book on the subject, he sent Lee Robertson an advance copy; Dr. Robertson read it, and the next Sunday morning at his church in Chattanooga, he preached a sermon condemning Hollywood movies. That was in 1955, 57 years ago. Heard any sermons on the subject lately? And yet, I say again, what they're putting out today are infinitely worse than the movies Dr. Robertson was condemning in 1955.

Then it mentions, "craftsmen, of whatsoever craft." The Greek word translated "craftsmen" is *technites,* from which we get our word "technician." In Acts chapter 19, where it talks about Demetrius the silversmith, who led a riot against Paul, it twice calls him a *technites,* a craftsman. And in Hebrews 11:10, where it says that Abraham "looked for a city which hath foundations, whose builder and maker is God," the word translated "builder" is *technites.* And in chapter 18 of Acts, where it talks about Paul making tents, it uses the same word.

So the meaning is, somebody who's making something, whether it's a statue of Diana, or a tent, or God creating heaven. And John says that all such activity is going to cease - think of Bill Gaither's song, *The King Is Coming* - one of the things he says will happen is "all the builder's tools are silent."

Then he says, there will be "no more sound of the millstone." We talked about mills last week, so perhaps it's not necessary to spend a lot of time on this point - but it represents the world of commerce and trade - as I told you last week, that day in time - as, indeed, around here 150 years ago, the mill was the biggest business in town. John's meaning is, that all commerce us going to come to a halt.

Then he says that there will be no more "light of a candle." The better word is "lamp" rather than "candle," and all the new translations so translate it. I'll go a bit farther and say that this is one place where the new translations may be an improvement on the KJV - and I doubt that I've ever said that before, either up here, or anywhere else. But these kids from the seminary, who think they know it all, you ask them, "OK, show me a place where the new version is right and the KJV is wrong," has any of them ever gone to Rev. 18:22, and said, "Here's an example." No, and I've been asking people the question for fifty years. None of these kids from the Seminary have any clue what they're talking about.

Then it says, there will no more be heard, "The voice of the bridegroom and the voice of the bride." Perhaps that's intended simply to suggest that all joyful celebrations will come to an end. But elsewhere in the New Testament, it tells us that, at the end of the age, the institution of marriage will be under attack. So I think we may fairly read this as meaning that, at the time John's talking about, normal family relations will cease.

Today, 40% of white children in the United States, and 70 % of all black children, are born out of wedlock. Folks live together, and have kids together, without ever getting married. Doesn't that suggest that, even in today's world, "the voice of the bridegroom and of the bride" has ceased, to a large degree. One of the greatest problems facing America today, is the decline of the family. I've talked about it before, and I've talked about it frequently, so I won't spend the rest of the hour on it tonight - although I'm tempted to. But coming events cast their shadows, and I believe the decline in the American family, is a precursor of worse to come, and a sure sign that we're living in the last days.

Now, the last two verses of the chapter, verses 23 and 24, tell us why God's destroyed Babylon. Why'd He do it? We don't have to guess, and we don't have to speculate, because He gives us the reasons, in so many words. Look at the last half of verse 23: " for thy merchants were the great men of the earth; for by thy sorceries were all nations deceived. And in her was found the blood of prophets, and of saints, and of all that were slain upon the earth.." Why'd God destroy Babylon? Why's God going to destroy the world system? Three reasons are given.

First, because "thy merchants were the great men of the earth." You say, so what? Businessmen are usually important people in the community. At the present time, we have one who's trying to buy the Presidency; and so far, he's spent seventy of eighty million dollars in the attempt. Here's what I think the passage means. The great men in Babylon were who? Not the preachers. Not the educators. Not the philanthropists. The great men were, the merchants. The first sin it names, perhaps because it's more important than the other two, is materialism. Covetousness.

Is that true in America today? Isn't that what the schools are teaching our kids - "Money is the principal thing, therefore get money?" - to paraphrase Solomon's dictum. As Bro. Charles mentioned last Sunday, even many churches have been infected by the virus of materialism. That's what the prosperity gospel is all about - it's about getting people to give a lot of money to the church. That's not been the historical message of the church. My father-in-law, who's been in heaven for more than 25 years now, was a Baptist preacher. He preached in Southern Kentucky for 50 years.

I asked June recently, when she'd been listening to one of the prosperity preachers - I've forgotten which one - but I asked her, "June, you grew up under Pa's preaching. Is that what he preached?" And she said, "No, of course not. They didn't preach that way, back then, It was Oral Roberts who developed the principle of 'seed faith.' " I'm not slamming Oral Roberts - I don't know whether June's right, or not - maybe somebody else thought it up. But it's an extremely popular message today; and it's a radical departure from what has historically been the message of the church.

The second reason God says that He destroyed Babylon was because: "by thy sorceries were all nations deceived." Sorcery is not a word that we use in our everyday conversation. The Greek word so translated is *pharmakeia,* from which we get our word "pharmacy." One commentator explains the connection between drugs, which is the most obvious meaning of the word, explains its connection to false religion, as follows: "In 'sorcery,' the use of drugs, whether simple or potent, was generally accompanied by incantations and appeals to occult powers, with the provision of various charms, amulets, etc., professedly designed to keep the applicant or patient from the attention and power of demons, but actually to impress the applicant with the mysterious resources and powers of the sorcerer."

But in the context of the last days, it means tricks, impostures, false pretenses, deceptive maneuvers of all sorts. In Exodus, Pharoah's magicians are said, repeatedly, to have been engaged in "sorcery." So I believe it means "false religion." I think that's what's being pushed at us in America, from every direction. You've heard me say before that the religion of America is secular humanism - which means, we've cast God aside, cast His Word aside, and put man, and human reason in the position of ultimate authority. I think that's what the popular media are pushing today. I think that's what public schools and colleges are preaching. It's what liberal churches are preaching. How many of the churches out there, are doing what we're doing up here, trying to get men saved, expounding the Bible, week by week? Not many, and as time goes on, it's going to get worse. And that's one of the reasons God says that He's going to destroy the present, wicked world system - because it has rejected Him and His word, and elevated human reason above all.

The third reason God is destroying the world system is, verse 24, because "in her was found the blood of prophets, and of saints, and of all that were slain upon the earth." I've told you all along, ever since we've been studying the vision about the destruction of Babylon, chapters 17 and 18, I've said repeatedly, Babylon's not just Rome, either pagan or papal; it's not the literal city of Babylon; it represents the entire ungodly world system. And here's where it says it - at least by implication.

The verse says that Babylon has been responsible for the deaths of "all that were slain upon the earth." Now, as bad as pagan Rome was, it did not cause all the deaths of God's saints who were persecuted, from the beginning of the world until that time. As bad as the Roman Catholic Church was - and I had ancestors who were French Hugenots, and were forced to flee from Europe to North Carolina, to avoid persecution by the Catholic Church - but as wicked as the Catholic Church has been, it didn't cause all the deaths of every saint who was persecuted since the beginning of time. The wicked, ungodly, Satanic world system did - and that's what Babylon represents. That's the only way the verse makes any sense.

Now, it says she's persecuted the "prophets." Thayer's Lexicon defines the term as meaning: "One upon whom the Spirit of God rested, one to whom and through whom God speaks. In the case of the Old Testament prophets their messages were very largely the proclamation of the Divine purposes of salvation and glory to be accomplished in the future; the "prophesying" of the New Testament "prophets" was both a preaching of the Divine counsels of grace already accomplished, and the foretelling of the purposes of God in the future." The prophets were both foretellers - which is what we usually think of when the word is used; but they were also forthtellers - and I think in this context it means simply, the public teachers of the true religion.

It also says that Babylon persecuted "the saints." All through the book of Revelation, we've encountered this word - here, it means simply, the saved people on earth. All through the book, we've seen, for five years now, passage after passage about this world persecuting the saints. This is the last time it says it. The next time the word occurs, in verse 8 of the next chapter, chapter 19, the church is in heaven at the marriage supper of the Lamb. Job said, immediately upon losing his family and having been afflicted with boils - he talked about a place where, he said: "There the wicked cease from troubling; and there the weary be at rest."

One day there's going to come an end to persecution. One day the public schools are going to be closed down, and the teachers are all going to face God's judgment for what they've done by destroying America's kids and making atheists of them. One day Child Protective Services will be out of business, and every social worker who's persecuted Christian parents will stand before the judgment bar of God. One day all the liberal clergy and seminary professors, who've taken the penknife of higher criticism and cut the heart out of the Word of God, are going quit sending souls to hell, and will have to explain to God why they did it. And that's the day we're looking forward to.

I'm going to stop there - I could run on much longer on that point, and I will, in the weeks to come. This takes us to the end of chapter 18; so go home and read chapter 19, and then come back next week, and we'll begin the chapter that ends with the second advent of Jesus Christ.

About the author:

William L. Turner, currently a resident of Bardstown, Kentucky, has been a Baptist pastor, district missionary, college instructor, and attorney for more than half a century. Dr. Turner holds a Ph.D. in Educational Administration from the University of Wisconsin-Madison, and a J.D. from Indiana University-Bloomington School of Law. He is married, and has seven children, and fifteen grandchildren. He welcomes your input and suggestions - turn4299@gmail.com.

Printed in Great Britain
by Amazon

64604128R00090